This book is dedicated to Kit, Bea, Samuel and Izzie—a new generation of budding songwriters ... Carry the torch far kids!

HOW [NOT] TO WRITE A HIT SONG!

101 COMMON MISTAKES TO AVOID IF YOU WANT SONGWRITING SUCCESS

Brian Oliver

TABLE OF CONTENTS

# # # #

INTRODUCTION

"I tried to look at writing a song almost like solving a mystery. The song was there, buried somewhere in my brain. All I had to do was follow the clues until I figured it out"
—Jon Skovron, author, *Struts & Frets*

SOMEONE once said, "All great songs are unique, but all bad songs are the same". It's also true to say that all bad songs share common faults.

The purpose of this book is to identify and highlight many of the most common songwriting errors so that you can try to avoid them in your own songs.

If it's important to learn from your mistakes, it's even better to learn from someone else's…

That's why this is more of a 'How Not To' book rather than just another 'How To' book on songwriting.

There are many excellent publications about songwriting theory, song construction, chord theory, the craft of lyric writing and so on. And there are many heavyweight tomes that can teach you the language and notation of music and the theory of composition.

But you don't need any note-reading ability or a knowledge of chord numbers and the like to be able to follow this book. The content is presented in a way that is designed to make it easy and quick to digest, even if you only play by ear.

That's because you don't have to be able to read and write music to create great songs.

Hit songwriters who have done okay without music notation skills include John Lennon, Paul McCartney, Jimi Hendrix, Brian Wilson, Stevie Wonder, Neil Diamond, and Irving Berlin (in fact, Berlin could only play the piano in one key).

Whether you read music or not, there are a number of key components that are consistently found in the structure, melodies and lyrics of all hit songs. This book analyzes the errors that are commonly made when building these various elements into a song.

When a new idea suddenly hits you—and all the pieces drop into place so quickly that the song almost writes itself—it's very easy to fall into the trap of rushing straight into a studio and recording a demo. You then confidently submit the song to a music publisher or record company believing it's the best thing you've ever written—only to suffer the agony of having the song rejected.

Sometimes it is best just to slow down, take a step back, and re-examine each element of your new song. If you don't spend a little more time polishing it, there is a danger that it may still contain some weaknesses that you failed to spot first time around. A new song often needs several re-writes before you have the final version.

That's why one of the purposes of this book is, in effect, to give you a detailed checklist that you can measure each of your own songs against, no matter how 'finished' you think they are. The aim is to help you develop your own unique writing style while avoiding fundamental mistakes at each key stage in the song development process.

The research for this book has highlighted many frequent causes of songwriting problems—from having the wrong mental attitude and an unsatisfactory songwriting environment … to common mistakes in the basic construction of songs. From getting the blend of core ingredients wrong, to flawed choices when it comes to song titles, melodies, lyrics, hooks, choruses, intros, bridges, pre-choruses …and even the demo itself.

Music companies have been going through major changes in recent years. With music buyers now able to download only the individual songs that they really like, the music industry has become a singles market again—and pop is once more the dominant force.

As a result, there are once again great opportunities for new songwriters who are capable of crafting hit singles with memorable melodies and lyrics that touch everyone who hears them. This applies whether you're writing songs for yourself as a self-contained artist, or for your own band, or for other artists.

Gone are the days when an artist could get away with releasing an album that included only a couple of hits and the rest of the tracks were just uninspiring 'fillers'. These days, if artists want audiences to shell out cash for an entire album, they have to include a generous helping of hit songs on the album.

Even major artists can't simply release 'album tracks' any more. Everybody is looking for hit songs.

This means music publishers, A&R executives, record producers and artist managers have become even hungrier for new writers who can come up with exceptional songs to fill the slots that artists and their producers can't fill themselves.

At the same time, though, competition is intense and music industry standards are set very high. So it's more important than ever to avoid the pitfalls that other new songwriters fall into—and make sure your songs are the best, and stand out from the crowd.

I should emphasize that this book is primarily aimed at writers who want to create self-contained songs—the kind of songs that still sound great when it's just one singer and one instrument playing them in any music genre. So we're not talking about songs that are 'productions' which can't be replicated without all the latest studio frills and gimmicks.

Despite the proliferation of digital technology, Billy Steinberg—co-writer of hits such as Madonna's 'Like A Virgin', 'True Colors' by Cyndi Lauper, The Bangles' 'Eternal Flame' and 'So Emotional' by Whitney Houston—believes the music industry is increasingly turning to talented songwriters again.

"Even though there are some songs, especially heavy rap or dance songs, that are more about the track and computer-driven music, I think it's coming back around," Steinberg said in 2013. "I think there are more real songs written in the last 12 months than the previous five years."

I hope this book will help to guide you and your songs along the bumpy (but exciting and potentially rewarding) path to songwriting success.

Good luck!

Brian Oliver
March 2013

# # # #

PART 1:

GETTING STARTED

#1
DON'T THINK SONGWRITING IS EASY

"Performing is the easiest part of what I do, and songwriting is the hardest."
—Neil Diamond

IF YOU see songwriting as an easy way to get rich quick, you'll need to think again if you really want to achieve success.

Let's be clear, songwriting is not easy. And writing hit songs is even harder. As Jimmy Webb once observed: "Songwriting is hell on Earth. If it isn't, then you're doing it wrong."

Sure, there are many hit songwriters who make it look easy. We've all heard about writers who finished a song in the time it takes to boil an egg and it went on to earn a fortune. Country legend Hank Williams used to say: "If a song can't be written in 20 minutes, it ain't worth writing". Lady Gaga wrote her first single 'Just Dance' in 10 minutes—the same length of time it took the Beach Boys' Bruce Johnston to write the Barry Manilow classic 'I Write the Songs'.

The truly great songwriters just make it look easy. In reality, though, they have to put in hundreds of hours of hard work—making many mistakes along the way—in order to hone their talent and achieve their greatness. Diane Warren, one of the most successful female songwriters of all time, spent 20 years writing six days a week, 10-12 hours a day before she felt she could finally take the occasional weekend off!

The legendary lyricist Sammy Cahn once explained: "Writing a song can be agony or ecstasy. It can take half an hour or half a year."

That's why it's important to understand that hit songwriting is a process. It's an art and a craft.

The initial spark that ignites your song idea is a gift. From then on, it's all about hard work. With the majority of successful songs, the first draft is just the beginning—only the first of many in the evolution of the song. It took Janis Ian three months to write her classic track 'At Seventeen'.

Don't forget, songwriting is also a business. Music publishers and record company A&R representatives are highly selective because they are there to make money and hang on to their jobs. So your songs must be commercially viable. They not only have to compete with what's already out there in the marketplace, they have to be BETTER.

All of which calls for an exceptional level of self-motivation and self-belief, as well as talent. The desire to create, excel, and be the best has to come from deep within you. You have to be willing to do whatever it takes to achieve the success you desire.

As Diane Warren says: "You've got to believe, then work hard at it".

# # # #

#2
DON'T EXPECT MIRACLES

"If you have faith in your ability, never give up. I was writing songs for eight years before I met with any success. Learn from your mistakes and keep trying"
—Ellie Greenwich

AS A music publisher, one of the biggest mistakes I see talented new songwriters make is to expect something to happen with every song they write—and then get disillusioned and give up when it doesn't happen.

It's important to recognize that, when you're first starting out, each song you write is just a stepping-stone to the next one. It's all part of an important learning process that gradually takes you closer to finding your own 'voice' and your own distinctive writing style.

So be persistent. You may have to write 30 or more songs—and endure the heartbreak of many failed demo submissions—before you come up with your first 'breakthrough' song capable of having a real chance of success. Many top songwriters admit that they ended up throwing away their first 50 or so songs because they just weren't good enough.

Barry Mann and Cynthia Weill—who wrote the classic '(You've Lost) That Loving Feeling'—admit that their earliest songs weren't all great. As Barry Mann told the *Huffington Post*: "If we looked at a list of a hundred songs we wrote, going back even to the Sixties and Seventies, the first twenty-five weren't so good, then all of a sudden number twenty-six, number twenty-seven, number twenty-eight and twenty-nine were really terrific songs. Not all of our songs were great songs, but at that point, we were learning."

Some writers find it hard to get started on a new song because they're afraid of failing or ending up with a really bad song. However, as Canadian poet and novelist Margaret Atwood once remarked: "If I waited for perfection, I would never write a word."

To achieve your goals you need to have the courage to face rejection and the self-belief, passion and perseverance to keep going. Be ambitious and constantly challenge yourself in terms of song construction, genres, and the subjects you write about. But set realistic expectations. Don't expect miracles.

Award-winning country music songwriter Brett James believes in the so-called '10,000-Hour Rule'. He explains: "The rule says that it takes 10,000 hours of practice to master anything. I feel this can apply to songwriting too. It takes about 10,000 hours of writing to become skilled at it."

As the legendary Brian Wilson once said: "No masterpiece ever came overnight. A person's masterpiece is something that you nurture along."

# # # #

## 3

NOT KNOWING YOUR JOB DESCRIPTION

"Whenever I fill out the job description I put 'songwriter', never 'singer' or
'artist'. Singers come and go"
— Brian McKnight

WHEN STARTING any new job, you are more likely to be successful if you are given a proper description of what you're supposed to be doing ... and what you're expected to achieve.

Songwriting is no different, except it is down to you to define your role.

—Are you a composer? Or a lyricist? Or a songwriter who writes both words and music?

—Do you see yourself as a singer-songwriter?

—Are you writing songs for your own self-contained band?

—Do you want a career writing songs for other artists?

—Are you offering your services as a 'topliner', writing the melody and lyrics (the topline) for backing tracks created by dance DJs and producers?

—Do you aspire to co-write with writer/producers? (producers sometimes sign young writers to work with them in writing sessions)

—Are you a budding writer/producer yourself? Are you creating and recording songs for a new singer or band that you're nurturing?

Whatever your role is, your job description will probably read something like this: "Part creative genius, part tireless market researcher, and part 'never take no for an answer' salesperson".

SINGER-SONGWRITER OR BAND MEMBER
Jimmy Webb once said: "The people who are making money are the ones who are writing and singing their own songs."

If you're trying to sell yourself to record companies as a singer-songwriter—or as part of a band that performs its own material—you'll have to put a much greater emphasis on style and originality to help you stand out from the crowd. A&R executives don't usually like to chase trends (at least they don't admit it!), so you'll need to show that you can push the musical envelope and offer some longevity.

If you're doing the singing yourself, you need to be sure your voice is good enough (or distinctive enough). You'll also have to focus on getting gigs and performing live—so that music publishers and A&R reps can come along and see you if they're interested.

TOPLINER

Talented topliners are in short supply. But if you want to add this form of songwriting to your 'job description', be aware that DJ/producers and dance labels often send the same track to a multitude of topline writers. They ask them all to come up with a melody, hook and lyrics which can be laid over the musical soundbed that they have created. The producer then selects the one that he or she likes best.

If your topline isn't chosen, your efforts (and the cost of your demo) may have been wasted. You might not be able to use your primary melody for anything else because the chord progressions, riffs, beats, and instrumental sounds on the track are all owned by the producer. You may, however, be able to re-work your lyrics for another song.

SONG PROVIDER

If you're going to write for other artists, you'll have to learn how to tailor your songs (melodically and by subject matter) to meet the requirements of each artist you're targeting.

"If you're good at writing then you have to be able to do it in any genre," Emeli Sandé believes. "And if the production changes, the song can still stand."

This means doing plenty of research—including studying other songs by the artist, analyzing their vocal range, and writing songs in their style. You'll also have to find a way to get your song to the artist past 'gatekeepers' such as the artist's producer, personal manager, or A&R manager (more research!).

Be aware that it is common for major artists to demand songwriting credits on a track, even if the artist doesn't make any contribution to the writing. Songwriting pros jokingly refer to this as "change a word, get a third".

Diane Warren believes tenacity is vital if you're going to succeed as a song provider for other artists. "I'm the one who got my songs covered," she once said. "My dad was a salesman who didn't take 'no' for an answer. I'm kind of known as someone like that too. When I believe in something, I'm hardcore about it. You can't really turn me away."

# # # #

#4
NOT RECOGNIZING YOUR LIMITATIONS

"Every collaboration helps you grow"
—Brian Eno

AS A music publisher, I have often urged solo songwriters to consider collaborating with someone else in order to strengthen persistent weaknesses in their songs. Naturally, some writers have felt offended by such a suggestion.

You may feel that your creative process is so personal that you don't want to open it up and share it with anyone else. But the fact is, not all songwriters can be great composers *and* great lyricists. Sometimes a co-writer with talents that complement your own can help to take you and your songs to a much higher level.

Maybe you're writing well-constructed songs with great melodies but they're not being taken up because your lyrics are inferior. Without strong lyrics, you're going to have a tough time selling your songs. Or maybe you're great at coming up with catchy titles and imaginative lyrics but your musical abilities are limited.

If you only write melodies or only lyrics, why not consider co-writing if it means an average song can be turned into a potential hit?

A songwriting partner can help to keep you focused. He or she can question your lyrics when you're under-achieving, and introduce fresh ideas and new chords that may take your songs to new places.

And if you've got a great idea for a song but you just can't seem to finish it, a co-writer may be able to listen objectively to what you've got and come up with the missing link. He or she may introduce lyrical or melodic ideas that would never have occurred to you.

As Robbie Shakespeare of long-time reggae duo Sly and Robbie once remarked: "You have two sets of ears, you can hear more…".

English boy band phenomenon One Direction had an average of five pairs of songwriting ears per track on their hit 2012 album *Take Me Home*. In recent years, producers of pop artists who aren't also songwriters have found that the TV sitcom-style 'writers room' model is the best way to consistently generate hits. As a result, more pop writers now tend to work in teams.

Many top writers acknowledge that co-writing and building relationships with other writers is one of the best ways to grow as a songwriter. You may find that regular collaboration with various songwriters will help you to learn how to write better songs—faster.

Collaboration also makes good business sense. The more songwriters there are on a song, the more the song gets played and heard within the music industry.

Doors that were previously closed to you could soon start opening up if your co-writers already have publishing deals, or if they are record producers with a direct gateway to established artists.

# # # #

#5
NOT STICKING TO A DAILY WRITING SCHEDULE

"In my early 20s I used to sit down and force myself to write a song a day just to write something. They're horrible, but they're songs. Somewhere in your unconscious it's going in that you've finished something."
—Janis Ian

SOME WRITERS have the ambition and the talent to write hit songs, but they lack the determination and self-discipline to make it happen. It is important to challenge yourself to write something every day, even when you don't feel like it.

So don't keep making excuses for yourself, start writing. Otherwise your potential hit songs will never get written.

Establishing a consistent writing habit—making it part of your daily routine—will boost your creativity and productivity, and lead to better songs.

If you want to earn your living as a writer, it's important to remember that songwriting is a business—not a hobby. The professional songwriters you will be competing with write every day, turning out at least 100 new songs a year. So you need to do the same.

As top country songwriter Brett James explains: "I tell young songwriters that they should write 100 songs per year, then get 30 of these songs put on hold, then get 10 cuts per year to hopefully get one hit a year."

Think of it as running your own store. If you only open your doors when you feel like it, your shop isn't going to sell much. You need to be open for business every day.

"I go into my office every day and work," says Nick Cave. "Whether I feel like it or not is irrelevant."

PJ Harvey takes a similar view: "If you want to be good at anything, you have to work hard at it. It doesn't just fall from the sky. I work every day at trying to improve my writing, and I really enjoy it."

It is also important to identify the most creative time of day for you. For example, some people like to write something as soon as they wake up in the morning, when their mind is full of ideas. Are you an early bird? Or an afternoon person? Or a night owl?

Make your most fruitful hours your 'writing time', and get into the habit of sitting down and writing something at the same time every day (even if it's just for half an hour). If you can find this prime time and get writing, you'll be a lot more productive. You'll be amazed how the quality and volume of your songs will improve as a result.

"Music breeds its own inspiration", Burt Bacharach once remarked. "You can only do it by doing it. You may not feel like it, but you push yourself."

# # # #

#6
NOT HAVING A SPECIAL WRITING PLACE

TO MAINTAIN a daily writing schedule, it's important to find the ideal place at home where you can focus and be creative.

It should be a clutter-free zone where you feel most comfortable—with no distractions. A special place where you can close the door, turn off your phone, and give your mind the focused time it needs to get your creative juices flowing.

If you're one of those people who are addicted to social media, switch it off for a while. You don't have to check Facebook, Twitter, Pinterest and all the other potential time wasters every five minutes. You won't miss anything. But your songwriting could gain a lot from the time you save!

You may also find it motivating to have a writing space that is big enough to allow you to keep your essential tools—such as your instrument, digital recorder, rhyming dictionary, thesaurus, notebook, and laptop or tablet—in plain sight all the time.

If, like me, you're a guitarist, try keeping your guitar on a stand instead of hidden away in its case. Seeing the guitar may make you want to pick it up, play a few chords ... and, hey presto, a new song idea may hit you as a result!

# # # #

#7
NOT SETTING YOURSELF DEADLINES

"Having a deadline sharpens you"
—Robin Gibb

ACHIEVING SUCCESS as a songwriter is about being highly focused and productive as well as having the necessary talent and ability to craft hit songs. That means giving yourself clear objectives—and sticking to them.

For example, try setting yourself monthly, weekly or daily songwriting targets—such as 'finish four new songs this month' ... 'complete one verse every day' ... or 'write a song this week using a chord I haven't tried before'. Write these goals down and pin them up in your writing room as a reminder of what you're trying to achieve.

The feeling of knowing that you've hit your target is a great motivator. But make sure your goals are achievable.

In an interview with *Music Week* magazine, the Bee Gees' Robin Gibb emphasized the benefits of working to a deadline: "I know a lot of people don't like pressure, but it works," he said. "If you've only got a certain amount of time to write something, you will come up with it. And it's amazing how you focus and get inspired if you know there is a limited amount of time."

He pointed out that the Bee Gees were given a very tight deadline when they were asked to write the music for Saturday Night Fever. "We ended up writing 'How Deep Is Your Love', 'Night Fever', 'Stayin' Alive' and 'If I Can't Have You' all in one week," he said.

# # # #

#8
NOT LAYING FOUNDATIONS FOR THE CREATIVE PROCESS

"Very often, ideas come to me when I'm falling asleep—when the busy mind gets out of the way, and the intuitive, imaginative mind gets a shot at the steering wheel"
—David Crosby

MOST SONGWRITERS have experienced the frustration of sitting down to write a new song, only to find that nothing comes, or what you do manage to write just isn't good enough.

There can be many reasons for this. Your mind may be on something else or maybe you're worried about something. Often, though, it's simply because you haven't prepared yourself properly for your writing session.

Experienced songwriters know that the creative process involves four key stages: (1) preparation, (2) incubation, (3) inspiration, and (4) realization.

Incubation is where an idea takes shape in your subconscious, like a program running in the background on your computer.

Inspiration is where an idea floats up from your subconscious and you seem to pluck it out of the air.

And **realization** is where the idea becomes a reality as you turn it into the first draft of a new song.

However, **Preparation** is the foundation stone of the entire creative process. But being 'prepared' to write a song doesn't just mean keeping your instrument, laptop, digital recorder and rhyming dictionary ready in your writing room just in case.

In songwriting, 'creative preparation' is a state of mind. It means being observant and keeping your mind constantly open for new ideas through your experiences, thoughts, feelings and observations. It means keeping your songwriter's antenna switched on to the world around you at all times.

An idea for a title or a lyric line can come from overhearing a conversation on a train or in a café … or an event that you witness … or while you're waiting at a traffic light. Similarly, a headline in a newspaper, on a website, or on a poster might spark an idea for a song.

I remember sitting in a bar with one of my songwriters, Steve Thompson, and we were discussing how to generate new ideas for songs. We spotted a vintage 1930s travel poster on the wall with the headline: *Paris By Air*. A few weeks later Steve had written a song called 'Paris By Air' which went on to be a hit for a leading British rock band!

One of the hardest things about songwriting is having to start with a blank page. But it is often easier to find inspiration if you have already laid the creative foundations by having a list of 'ready-made' ideas you can dip into—with many of the ideas based on your real-life experiences and observations.

# # # #

#9
LETTING GOOD IDEAS GET AWAY

"If I knew where the good songs came from I'd go there more often"
—Leonard Cohen

GREAT SONG titles, topics and lyric lines can come from anything and everything around you. So always be prepared to grab them as they come up.

In the same way that a photographer always needs to carry a camera, you should always keep a pen and a notebook with you. Or, like Taylor Swift, Max Martin and REM's Michael Stipe, use the voice memo/notebook option on your phone to capture ideas for themes, lyrics or melody lines before you forget them.

As Paloma Faith told *American Songwriter* magazine: "I like going through life with a notebook in my pocket or a notebook on my phone. Sometimes I hear somebody say something on the street. I like to capture a sentence and it resonates and takes on a different meaning for me."

Make a note of phrases that you hear or read in newspapers and magazines, and create sketches of these potential songs.

And make sure you're well organized. Maintain a list of ideas for titles and hooks. Keep them safe in a digital folder or a physical workbook or 'Ideas' file, along with other unfinished songs, melody lines and lyrics.

It is important to keep all of these odds and ends in one place so you always know where to find them. Coming back to them at a later date—and looking at them from a fresh perspective—can often result in a spark of inspiration that helps you finish the song. Sometimes the best songs just need to gestate a little in your subconscious before all the pieces fit together.

The Bee Gees' Robin Gibb always believed in "keeping the tape running" during the writing process—even if a writing session doesn't seem to be going well.

"You never know when you're going to come up with something and then if you'll remember it completely," said Gibb.

"All the ideas, everything, will be on tape and then you can always refer back at any time," he added. "Melodies will be born for the first time during writing and unless you have it on tape you haven't got any way of remembering them."

Don't make the mistake of letting good song ideas get away just because you're a little disorganized.

# # # #

#10
BAD ORGANIZATION

IF YOU want to make a living as a writer, it's important to remember that songwriting is a business—not a hobby. That means you have to get your act together and be as well-organized, focused and professional as anyone else who is running their own business.

Unfortunately, getting organized is often a significant weak spot for writers—and it's a failing that could affect your chances of success.

The need for 'good organization' may seem to have little to do with your ability to write great songs. Nevertheless, it is a key part of building a successful and productive songwriting process. A messy writing space, for example, can clutter your mind and hamper your creativity.

That's why it's important to have a system that enables all your new song ideas and unfinished melodies and lyrics to be stored in one place (either digitally or physically) so you won't lose them. Otherwise, you run the risk of a potential future hit song remaining unwritten!

It is equally important to have a good digital or physical filing system for the songs and demos that you have completed so you can access them quickly.

Nobody likes doing all that boring paperwork and filing. But it is important to be clutter-free by keeping all of your correspondence and important documents (such as contracts and royalty statements) in separate folders—ideally with a different color code for each folder category so you can find them easily. And make sure you keep your physical folders in a good old fashioned filing system, including a filing cabinet if you have space for one.

Timing is often a key factor when it comes to getting your songs heard by the right people in the music industry. What if you make a new publishing contact who is willing to listen to your songs, but you have to send a demo or an online link today because he or she is about to fly out of the country? What if you get a tip about an artist or a producer who urgently needs a particular type of song that perfectly matches one you've written? Are you sufficiently well-organized to be able to react quickly?

You could miss a golden opportunity if you find you can't instantly lay your hands on the relevant demo recording—or provide weblinks and lyric sheets—because you're filing system is in a mess!

# # # #

#11
NOT KEEPING YOUR WRITING STYLE CURRENT

"It's so important to know what's happening around you with records, radio, TV – everything. You've got to keep abreast of what's going on to stay on top of it all."
—Lamont Dozier

SONGWRITING IS a living thing. It continues to evolve with each new generation of artists and music. So it's vital to make sure you are creating songs that sound current and will appeal to today's audiences. Don't make the mistake of writing songs that could have been a hit 20 or 30 years ago.

If your songs don't sound like they belong on today's radio stations, music TV channels, or online music streaming services, you'll never be able to achieve any success with them. Remember, you're competing with today's top professional writers.

Wayne Hector—writer of number one hits around the world for artists such as Britney Spears, One Direction, Susan Boyle, The Wanted and Enrique Iglesias—warns new songwriters about the importance of keeping up to date. "If you do a record that's for a younger crowd," he says, "the thing that happens as a writer is a lot of the time the sound changes and what's young is not what was young back in the day so you're displaced. You no longer recognize what constitutes a hit now."

The best way to keep your own writing fresh is to study and analyze what today's hit songwriters are doing. Listen to what's being played on the radio. Buy chart CDs or download individual tracks from iTunes or streaming services like Spotify or Deezer.

Instead of buying the sheet music, try working out the chords by ear. It will help you to understand how the writer felt when he or she was searching for the right chord in crucial parts of the song. Figuring out the chord progressions by yourself will give you a much better idea of how current songs are constructed.

You'll find there are standard forms around which most songs are organized today.

Take notes on the other components that current hit songs have in common—such as their rhyming structure and the melodic elements that provide a contrast between verse and chorus. Then apply what you learn to your own work … adding something original of your own, of course, to make it stand out from the crowd.

# # # #

#12
IMITATING INSTEAD OF INNOVATING

"Imitate, assimilate, and innovate."
—Clark Terry

MANY DEVELOPING songwriters either simply try to mimic what's already out there, or they try too hard to be different and end up writing in a form that many listeners just can't understand. You have to strike a balance between these two extremes.

To find receptive ears in the music industry (and amongst record buyers), your songs need to sound familiar—but not similar.

If you're trying to get a record deal for your band, or for yourself as a singer-songwriter, major labels will tell you they want something distinctive and different that makes you stand out from the pack.

At the same time, though, your music has to be familiar enough to be commercial and marketable so that it will sell (which, at the end of the day, is all that record companies and publishers are really interested in). A hint of familiarity helps people relate to your songs.

The same criteria apply if you plan to sell your music direct to fans through your own website or via online music retailers such as iTunes, Amazon and CDBaby. To achieve maximum success, you need to appeal to the many not just the few.

So don't try to sound like someone else … but don't try too hard not to!

Music industry executives talk about the need for new artists to create their own style. But what they really mean is they want you to sound original, but your songs should not be completely different from anything they've ever heard before.

They want something that develops what is already out there—not a sudden leap that leaves a huge gap between you and the audience. 'Style' evolves constantly over time; it is rarely revolutionary.

When asked what steps should be taken to achieve musical success, the great trumpet player Clark Terry famously replied: "Imitate, assimilate, and innovate".

In other words, listen to what's being played on the radio today, analyze current trends, absorb the key elements of current hit songs, emulate them—then carve your own niche by innovating and adding something new of your own.

Hit songwriters are rarely born as great writers. They become great by learning from the great writers who preceded them.

Imitating successful songwriters that you admire is one of the surest ways of developing your own writing skills.

Analyze and dissect your heroes' songs by picking out the chord progressions by ear. This will give you a much better understanding of the building blocks used to create the songs and how the different sections are joined together. Similarly, analyze the lyrics for these songs and absorb the rhyming patterns and keywords used.

Then try writing your own songs based on these proven templates and chord progressions.

Through your subconscious assimilation of the shape, form and content of the songs that you're trying to copy, you'll find that you start adding something original of your own—such as new chord sequences. Your own songwriting style will soon begin to develop by building on what has gone before.

"When I was first learning songs," says Alicia Keys, "I'd have a favorite song, and I'd take the chords and twist them around. I'd learn the chords and then play them backward. That was my first experimenting with writing a song."

Jimmy Webb admits he also started out by "instinctively" imitating songs he heard on the radio. "How can you write an original song," he says, "if you haven't heard and 'read' at least a few of the most famous and best examples that have ever been written?".

That's how innovators like The Beatles and Hank Williams did it. John Lennon and Paul McCartney imitated and assimilated the songs of Little Richard, Chuck Berry, early Motown, Brill Building writers such as Gerry Goffin and Carole King, and R&B pioneers like Arthur Alexander. They found a way to do it differently and went on to change pop music forever.

As US Grammy award winner Boz Scaggs once remarked: "My songwriting and my style became more complex as I listened, learned, borrowed and stole and put my music together."

# # # #

#13
NOT GIVING MUSIC COMPANIES WHAT THEY WANT

WHETHER YOU'RE a singer-songwriter, a member of a self-contained band, or writing for other artists, your songs will only attract interest from music publishers, A&R reps, record producers and artist managers if you give them what they're looking for.

And what they're looking for is a single that is commercial enough to be played by mainstream radio.

The same criteria apply if you plan to sell your music direct to fans through your own website or via online music retailers such as iTunes, Amazon and CDBaby. To achieve maximum success, you need to have the broadest possible appeal.

Even in the 'connected' digital age of social media, YouTube, Vevo, blogging, online music streaming and mobile entertainment, good old radio airplay is still the key that can open the doorway to a big hit single.

Radio remains by far the main way consumers discover music, according to a 2012 study by research company Nielsen. The Nielsen consumer survey found that 48% of those questioned discover music most often through radio stations, compared with 10% from friends and relatives, 7% from YouTube, and around 4% from Spotify.

That's why what the music industry wants is the same as what the radio stations want.

For record labels, getting a single added to a radio station's weekly playlist is like winning a crucial football game every weekend.

All of which means you need to be constantly aware of what is currently being played on the radio. It is essential to take the commercial market—and the radio listener—into consideration when writing your songs. Don't just write for yourself.

# # # #

14
THINKING YOUR SONG TO DEATH

"I try, to the best of my ability, not to think the song to death"
—Robbie Robertson

IN ATTEMPTING to show how clever they are, many new writers try too hard and end up cramming too much into a song—making it way too long and unnecessarily complicated, and leaving the listener feeling confused.

Avoid over-thinking or over-writing your songs. Sometimes, the chords, melodies and lyrics that come to you instinctively are the right ones, so don't spend forever searching for the perfect melody or words.

In other words, know when to quit.

That's something Dave Matthews admits he finds hard to do.

"I take it too far sometimes," Matthews once told *Rolling Stone* magazine. "When I listen to my favorite songwriters, they have such simple melodies and chords. I occasionally manage to stop at the right time, but all too often I keep on going until I have way too many notes and words."

If you try to force too many messages into one song, you could end up overloaded with verses. Stephen Stills has always felt that writers should not be afraid to take a pair of scissors to their songs. "If I've got too many verses," he said, "I'll cut out two verses and then take the meaning of the song and condense it."

A hit song tends to comprise just one story told from one point of view. So stay focused. If you have several unrelated points that you want to get across to listeners, try putting them in separate songs.

And don't try to be too tricky with your chord progressions. Just concentrate on creating music and lyrics that can hold the listener's attention, and write a melody that is easy for them to remember.

In short, don't sabotage your songs by being too smart for your own good.

# # # #

#15
LIMITING THE APPEAL OF YOUR SONG

"I don't see anything wrong with being commercial. I think it's a gift"
—Janis Ian

IT IS important to strike a balance between creating a song that is inventive, fresh and original, but still easy for people to listen to and remember. This is true even if you're using your songs to define a distinctive musical identity for your own band, or for yourself as a singer-songwriter.

Your songs must be able to reach out and touch people without listeners having to struggle to understand what the song is all about.

The great Irving Berlin once remarked: "My ambition is to reach the heart of the average American, not the highbrow nor the lowbrow but that vast intermediate crew which is the real soul of the country ... My public is the real people."

New writers sometimes try too hard to show how clever and different they are in order to impress "the highbrow". As a result, their songs often end up being over-complicated, meandering and self-indulgent. And therefore easily forgotten.

If your aim is to earn a living as a songwriter, your songs need to have broad commercial appeal. If they contain elements that are common to a number of musical genres, your songs are likely to appeal to many different types of fans—and your success won't depend on just one artist or one genre.

If your song works 'unplugged' style with just one voice and one acoustic guitar or piano, there's a good chance it can easily be re-arranged and performed by artists in a number of different genres. Singers or bands can then take the elements of your song that are common to their particular corner of the market and make the song relevant to their own fans.

That's how songs become 'standards'.

There are countless examples of classic songs that were originally written for a specific musical style, but ended up being re-interpreted and recorded by artists from many different genres. From Ella Fitzgerald's swing version of Lennon & McCartney's 'Can't Buy Me Love' and Paul Anka's take on Van Halen's 'Jump' ... to Carrie Underwood's country version of 'Fix You' by Coldplay and Vanilla Fudge's psychedelic reworking of Holland-Dozier-Holland's 'You Keep Me Hanging On' (Brian Holland's favorite version of the song!).

The broader the appeal of your song—and the more cover versions that are available in the marketplace—the more money you'll earn from it!

# # # #

#16
YOUR TITLE DOESN'T INSPIRE

"A great title can inspire a song"
—Robin Gibb

STRONG AND interesting titles lead to stronger and more interesting songs because they inspire you to write better.

Once you find a great title, a song can almost write itself, or at least give you the direction that the song should take. It can help you to focus your creativity by defining the message of the song in a simple phrase or even just a single word.

Good titles are frequently action words, images or phrases that suggest other phrases which subsequently help the song to develop.

Intriguing and attention-grabbing titles are also essential to make your songs stand out when you submit your demos. A strong title can go a long way toward ensuring that music publishers, A&R reps and record producers remember your song.

Many publishers expect the majority of songs they receive from new writers to be unusable. They get hundreds of songs each week with uninspiring titles such as 'I Love You' and 'I Miss You'. You'll never get into the 'must-listen-to' pile if your title is just like every other song in the publisher's morning mail.

Many experienced writers don't even start working on a song until they have a great title that inspires them. They know the title is going to be the heart of the song. It will be their chorus and their hook. From that point on, writing the song becomes a process.

In an interview with *Music Week* magazine, Robin Gibb said the Bee Gees often focused on one-word song titles like 'Tragedy', 'Emotion' and 'Heartbreaker'.

"They're titles that say something without saying everything," said Gibb. "We've written whole songs from just getting a title like 'You Win Again', 'Islands In The Stream', 'Woman In Love', 'Chain Reaction' and 'Too Much Heaven'."

He added: "We came up with the titles for 'Too Much Heaven' and 'Tragedy' in an afternoon and wrote the songs the same day."

# # # #

#17
STOP WRITING 'ALBUM TRACKS'

"I don't do albums any more ... I do songs"
— Prince

UNLESS YOU'RE simply writing songs as a hobby, don't waste your time on self-indulgent 'album tracks'. These days, even established artists are finding it hard to sell albums—so album cuts won't earn you much in royalties.

It is vital to make every song you write so distinctive, original and commercial that it is a potential hit single. This applies whether your ambition is to achieve major success as a singer-songwriter, or as a member of a self-contained band, or as a professional song provider for other artists.

Trying to write an album full of singles doesn't mean the songs have to be formulaic 'throwaway' pop tunes. But they should be interesting, memorable and, most importantly, likely to get played on the radio! That's what record companies want to hear.

The growth of digital downloads means the music industry is once again a 'singles market' – just as it was between the 1950s and 1980s.

Throughout the 1990s, record companies tended to treat singles as 'samplers' to help promote their artists' albums. Today, sales of digital singles are increasing while overall album sales are falling.

As Lady Gaga's manager Troy Carter observed in 2012: "It's not an albums business anymore. It's a singles business...".

So don't write album tracks, write singles. They'll also earn you more in performance income if they get played on radio!

# # # #

#18
NOT DOING ENOUGH RESEARCH WHEN WRITING FOR OTHER ARTISTS

"You can be the best artist in the world, have the best production, but if you cut a bad song it's just a bad song with an incredible production"
—Don Williams

AS A music publisher, I have often received songs from writers (even experienced writers) with a note saying: "I wrote this song especially for so and so". Quite often, this is a complete waste of time if the artist concerned writes all of his or her own material.

I've also received songs where the melody line not only exceeded the vocal range of the intended artist, but also that of most other singers. This immediately limits the number of people who might conceivably be able to cover the song (one and a half octaves seems to be the maximum range for most singers).

To avoid making these mistakes—and wasting valuable songwriting ideas—you've got to spend time doing your homework.

Tailoring songs for a specific artist requires a methodical approach and thorough research.

It is important to get all the information you can about the artist you're targeting. Most importantly, check the writing credits on their records to make sure they don't write all their own songs. If they don't, there's a chance they may be open to high-quality outside material.

No matter how much you can hear the artist performing your song in your head, a publisher is unlikely to sign the song if they know the intended artist won't even consider anything by other writers. And if the song is too closely identifiable with that artist's style, a publisher might not be able to get anyone else to record it either.

If your target is an established artist, study the structure of their most successful records. Analyze the artist's vocal range. If you're pitching to a vocal group with several lead singers, take the sound of each singer into account. Also make sure the pacing of your lyrics gives artists plenty of room to style the song in their own unique way.

'Song casting' not only involves getting to know the artist's style, genre, vocal range and favored keys, but also the artist's audience. Your music and lyrics (and the sound and 'feel' on your demo) must be consistent with the artist's style … and what the artist's audience expects.

Swedish hit machine Max Martin—who has written hits for artists such as Taylor Swift, Britney Spears, Kelly Clarkson, Pink and Katy Perry—always conducts thorough research before writing tailor-made songs for artists. He goes to their live shows and finds out what kind of music they listen to at home. "I want the input because that makes the chemistry of the song," he says.

It's important to be aware that there are fewer song casting opportunities these days. If artists don't write their own songs, it's likely that their producers do. But there are always potential openings for great songs with exceptional melodies and lyrics that can reach out and touch people.

You just have to come up with songs that fill the repertoire gaps that artists and producers are unable to fill themselves.

Collaborations with artists are increasingly common these days as a way of getting songs covered. If an artist or a producer likes your song, they may want to make a few changes to suit the artist's style ... and thus become your 'co-writer'.

If the artist concerned sells millions of records, it may be worth giving up a share of your song for the money and the prestige – but don't sign anything before taking professional legal advice on how the copyright ownership and royalties should be split.

# # # #

#19
IGNORING THE 12 TESTS THAT DECIDE THE FATE OF YOUR SONG

"I can take criticisms but not compliments"
—James Taylor

CONTESTANTS on TV talent shows like *American Idol* and *The X-Factor* only have to face a panel of three or four judges, but your song will have to go through at least a dozen different judging panels on its way to being a chart hit.

Here are the 12 'jurors' who will ultimately decide your fate as a hit songwriter:

1. Your fellow **band members or musicians** who will play on your demo. They must decide whether the song is worthy of their best efforts in the studio or on stage.

2. A **music publisher** must judge the commercial viability of your song and decide whether they can make money by (a) helping you or your band secure a recording contract or (b) pitching your song to an artist who might want to cover it.

3. A **record company A&R rep** must be convinced that your songs have the originality and commercial potential they're looking for before they'll consider offering you or your band a recording contract. Similarly, an A&R gatekeeper will judge whether your song is good enough to be offered to one of the other artists on their label.

4. A **record producer** must decide whether your song is outstanding enough for them to want to cut it (whether with you, your band or one of the producer's other acts). In the case of a potential cover version, the producer must also judge whether the song will blend in with the other tracks that he or she is working on with the artist.

5. An **artist manager**—the person responsible for guiding an artist's career—must judge whether your song fits the style and musical direction that the artist plans to take on their next record.

6. A **recording artist** must be moved by the song both personally and professionally to want to record it and perform it—and put their career on the line as a result.

7. A **record company label manager** must decide whether the artist's version of your song is strong enough to be one of the 10 or 12 tracks that will be included on the artist's next album. The label manager will also consider whether the track should be a single.

8. The record company's **promotions team** must judge whether the track will get played on key radio stations. They have to believe in the song in order to really get behind it, take it to the media, and promote it like crazy to secure airplay.

9. **Radio programmers** must be convinced the song is what their listeners want to hear before deciding whether to add it to their playlists.

10. **Television producers** must be so impressed by the song that they'll want to put you, your band, or the artist who covered the song, on their shows.

11. **Trade music buyers** for online retailers and bricks and mortar record stores will judge whether the track is commercial enough for them to stock it and promote the record in-store or on their website.

12. The **public**, of course, will pass final judgment. They must hear the song on radio or TV or online and love it enough to go out and buy the record … and perhaps recommend it to their friends via social media.

# # # #

PART 2:

**COMMON MISTAKES IN SONG
CONSTRUCTION**

#20
NOT UNDERSTANDING SONG STRUCTURE

"I like the rules of songwriting. They're the same for me as they were for George Gershwin or Cole Porter"
—Sting

DEVELOPING A successful song structure is an essential part of writing hit songs. It is the key to being able to communicate your songs effectively to listeners. Yet many new writers are often not consciously aware that songs have a structure at all.

It is important to understand that hit songs need a well-defined framework that will enable the song's basic components (verses, choruses, bridges and pre-choruses) to work together to hold the listener's interest.

There are also specific conventions that are consistently found in the chord progressions, melodies, lyrics, rhymes and construction of all hit songs. Regardless of the genre of music involved, these common elements help to keep fans of that genre interested.

This is because, over the years, listeners have subconsciously come to expect to hear certain elements in songs. Skilled use of these components is what gives your song shape, keeps the momentum going, and is central to making the song memorable.

Although there have been many changes in genres, sub-genres and 'sounds' over the years, the basic structure of pop songs has evolved only slightly since the late 1950s.

As a result, if your song doesn't have a familiar structure (or if any key ingredients are not used well in the crafting of the song), it won't feel right to listeners ... and they'll quickly lose interest.

In other words, listeners like it when song form is clear, predictable and easy to follow.

Some new writers tend to create their song structure by 'feel' as they write each song. But this often causes the song to lack the impact (and commercial appeal) that it might have had if it had been written within a familiar framework.

It is worth spending time dissecting some of today's biggest hits. Once you understand the key elements of their song structure—and you get to know what the different components do, and why—you'll be able to challenge yourself to take them a step further ... and start to follow your own voice in your songs.

# # # #

#21
FAILING TO GIVE YOUR SONG A WELL-BALANCED SHAPE AND FORM

"As soon as I find the form I can finish the song in my head"
—Mose Allison

MUSIC PUBLISHERS and A&R executives tend to judge the commercial potential of new songs on the basis of three key principles: style, originality, and shape and form.

While style and originality are key factors from a marketing perspective, it is often the song's form that plays a major role in gaining a positive response from the most important judge of all ... the listener.

Scientists say practically all laws of nature are based on symmetries, and symmetry is deeply ingrained in humans' inherent perception of everything—from physical objects ... to the shape of people's faces ... to the music we listen to.

Whether we realize it or not, the repetition of melody, rhyme and form in popular music helps to meet this subconscious desire for symmetry. It creates a sense of predictability that is reassuring and a source of comfort for the listener.

That's why your songs need a well-balanced shape and form that is clear and easy for listeners to follow. The symmetry and predictability will allow you to establish a solid base on which you can then create a few surprises without taking listeners too far out of their 'comfort zone'.

Unless you're writing jazz, avoid complicated song forms with intricate time signatures, chord progressions and phrasing patterns. They are more likely to be perceived as confusing rather than creative.

Even when a song comes to you spontaneously, perhaps resulting in a complete verse or chorus in a flash of inspiration, there is a still point at which you will have to decide which basic form to use in order to convey the song effectively to the listener.

"I write a lot from instinct," Janis Ian once said. "But as you're writing out of instinct, once you reach a certain level as a songwriter, the craft is always there talking to you in the back of your head…telling you when it's time to go to the chorus, when it's time to rhyme. Real basic craft."

# # # #

#22
NOT KNOWING THE BASIC ELEMENTS OF A HIT SONG

WHEN YOU analyze your favorite writers' songs, you will find there are five basic elements around which most of their songs are built:

- an intro
- the verse
- a pre-chorus
- a chorus
- a bridge (also known as a 'middle eight').

There are always variations, of course, but very few hit songs stray far from using one of these five well-established frameworks:

1. Verse, Chorus, Verse, Chorus, Verse, Chorus.

2. Verse, Chorus, Verse, Chorus, Bridge, Chorus.

3. Chorus, Verse, Chorus, Verse, Chorus.

4. Verse, Verse, Chorus, Verse, Chorus, Chorus.

5. Verse, Pre-Chorus, Chorus, Verse, Pre-Chorus, Chorus.

The second of these structures (Verse, Chorus, Verse, Chorus, Bridge, Chorus) is the most popular song form today. The melodic 'hook' and title line are usually built into the chorus. Some writers also include a pre-chorus or 'lift' that connects the end of the verse to the chorus itself.

INTRO

Most songs start with a four-bar introduction (or 'intro'), although some songs may open with the chorus or go straight into the first verse. The intro is usually a catchy melodic phrase or riff that establishes the feel and tempo of the song and prepares the listener for the first verse.

It is always best to create the intro as part of your song, rather than adlib it as an afterthought when recording your demo.

VERSE

The verse tells the story like a chapter in a book, with different words in each verse to drive the story forward.

Although some verses may have 12 bars or 16 bars, most verses in today's hit songs tend to have no more than eight lyric lines and are usually eight bars long (the eight bars often comprise three two-bar melodies with a slight variation in the fourth two-bar melody line).

PRE-CHORUS

Typically only four bars long, the pre-chorus (also known as a 'lift') is designed to add a burst of extra energy at the end of the verse. Its function is to suddenly lift the melody and propel the listener into the chorus.

CHORUS

The chorus is the part of the song that is meant to get stuck in the listener's head.

While the lyrics are usually the same in every chorus, it should be melodically different from the verse with different chord changes. The chorus must contain the song's title and melodic 'hook', and should repeat the title line almost like a catchphrase.

Most choruses are typically four bars or eight bars long, with no more than eight lines of lyrics.

The chorus usually follows a verse, but songs that famously begin with the chorus include The Beatles' 'Can't Buy Me Love', 'Imma Be' by the Black Eyed Peas and Pink's 'Get the Party Started'.

BRIDGE

The bridge or 'middle-eight' is a four-bar or eight-bar section that usually only appears once in a song. It is designed to provide a temporary release from the repetition of the verse and chorus. It usually contains a whole new melody, with up to four lines of new lyrics that continue to expand the song's storyline (sometimes with an ironic twist).

To give your song symmetry, each verse, pre-chorus, chorus and bridge should be the same length every time. Straying too far from these established frameworks can make a song's form sound confusing and the melody may lack a recognizable shape (and therefore won't stick in the listener's mind).

VERSE-REFRAIN FORM

While the majority of today's hit songs are based on the verse-chorus format, some songs still use the more traditional verse-refrain structure.

A refrain is similar to a chorus, but musically and lyrically it is used to resolve and end a verse, whereas a chorus begins a distinctively new music section. Some verse-refrain songs may also include a bridge section.

REFRAIN

A refrain is typically a two-line repeated statement placed at the end of a verse. It usually includes the title line and the lyrics comment on or summarizes the preceding verse.

The refrain section should play the same role as the all-important hook in the verse-chorus format. Melodically and lyrically it should be catchy and memorable so that it stands out, lets people know what the song is called, and gets inside the listener's head.

One of the most famous examples of a verse-refrain song is Paul Simon's 'Bridge Over Troubled Water'. The refrain at the end of each verse consists of the same line sung twice: "Like a bridge over troubled water I will lay me down".

# # # #

#23
TRYING TO AVOID A TRIED AND TESTED FORM

"Sometimes a vocal melody can sit on top of a simple progression in a way that makes the song special"
—Chris Whitley

SOME NEW songwriters believe they will attract more interest in their songs by deliberately setting out to avoid using an established commercial format.

However, experimenting with form is not a good idea when you're trying to break into the music industry. Attempting to avoid falling into a familiar format can often lead to strange-sounding, forced chord progressions that don't resolve correctly—and may leave the listener confused or unsettled.

Building your songs around one of the four tried and tested variations of the Verse-Chorus-Verse-Chorus-Bridge-Chorus form does not mean you're 'selling out'. Many great songwriters continue to use these proven formats. Why? Because they work.

So don't be put off by critics who say that using an established framework is just 'formula writing'. Developing a song within an accepted structure doesn't mean you can't add something fresh and original of your own.

The challenge is to write something remarkable that stands out musically and lyrically but doesn't break all the rules of song form. Being 'different' within a tried and tested format—something Lennon & McCartney frequently did in their early days—means your songs will still be meaningful to listeners.

# # # #

#24
NOT TAKING TIME TO LEARN HOW HIT SONGS WORK

TAKING TIME to dissect and analyze current hit songs is a great way to develop a better understanding of how these songs work and why they are so successful. You can then apply this knowledge to your own songs.

It will help you to sharpen your own songwriting instincts, and your songs will get better much faster as a result.

The first step in analyzing a current hit song is to identify each different melodic segment within the song. The simplest way to do this is to create a simple flowchart on a piece of paper.

Draw a separate box for each different section of melody that you hear. This will break the song down into a sequence of boxes in your chart and, in this way, show you how the song is constructed.

Taking the common Verse, Chorus, Verse, Chorus, Bridge, Chorus format, Box 1 is likely to be the first verse (so label it '1st Verse'). Box 2 will be the '1st Chorus'. Box 3 will be the '2nd Verse', followed by the '2nd Chorus' in Box 4. There may be a completely different melody in a third segment (so label Box 5 as 'Bridge'). The song may then return to another verse and chorus, or go straight into the chorus repeats at the end of the song.

Some songs may also feature a different melody in a short segment between the end of the verse and the beginning of the chorus (put this section into its own box titled '1st Pre-chorus', '2nd Pre-chorus', etc.).

Other songs may even start with the chorus.

Once you have your 'map' of the song, you can break it down even further. Count the bars in each separate segment and enter the number in the appropriate box. A verse section usually has eight bars or maybe 16, while a chorus typically comprises eight bars. Also time the length of each section in minutes or seconds and put this figure in the box.

Next, work out the chords for each section of the song by ear, and analyze other aspects— such as rhyming patterns and melodic shapes—to determine how and why these elements work so well.

In addition to showing you the predictable elements of basic song forms, this exercise will also highlight how occasional variations—such as extra bars or an unexpected chord change—can surprise listeners and make the song more memorable.

As well as dissecting other writers' songs as part of your learning process, it is also important to spend time putting pen to paper and sketching out a linear representation of your own new songs. By analyzing and mapping out your latest songs in this way, you will be able to compare them with the structure, timings, chord progressions and rhyming patterns of current hit songs.

This should help you to ensure that you have the right components in the right order—and in the right place.

# # # #

#25
FORCING THE DEVELOPMENT OF A SONG

"I don't write songs, songs write me"
—Sammy Cahn

TRYING TOO hard to make a song happen—force-feeding the songwriting process—rarely leads to great results. A song that is labored often lacks the emotion of something that comes to you naturally like a perfectly-formed idea that you just pluck out of the air (or, more accurately, out of your subconscious).

"If you don't try and force it, a song will find the proper moment to come to life," says Valerie Simpson who co-wrote classic songs such as 'Ain't No Mountain High Enough' and 'Solid (As a Rock)' with her husband Nickolas Ashford.

Stephen Stills also believes in not pushing things if you feel your efforts during a writing session are exhausted, or if you've got songwriting block. "I sit down and start playing the guitar, if nothing comes I put it down," he says. "If something comes I pursue it until I get bored. I know better than to force it."

His former bandmate Neil Young holds a similar view: "If you don't have an idea and you don't hear anything going over and over in your head, don't sit down and try to write a song. Go mow the lawn…".

When inspiration does come, don't stop the flow. Take the chords, melodies and lyrics that come instinctively and accept that they may change during the creative process. Don't go chasing the 'perfect' melody or rhyme or the correct phrasing – just get the first draft of the song written.

If you spend too much time trying to perfect one element of the song, you may lose your connection with the spark that ignited the idea in the first place.

Similarly, don't try to rush a new song. Be patient.

We've all heard the stories about classic songs that were written in 10 minutes, but the majority of well-crafted songs are actually the result of many rounds of re-writes and careful polishing.

English singer-songwriter Ed Sheeran told *American Songwriter* magazine that he'd spent five years working on a particular song. "This one song keeps evolving," he said, "and I keep adding bits to it."

If you find you're stuck with one of your songs, try sleeping on it. Scientists now believe that a nap can boost creative thought.

A study by researchers at the University of California in San Diego concluded that problems are more likely to be solved after a period of dreamy sleep. Scientists believe rapid eye movement (REM) sleep allows the brain to form new nerve connections without the interference of other thought pathways that occur when we are awake or in non-dreamy sleep.

Anecdotal evidence suggests there could be some truth in this. Paul McCartney has often spoken about the melody for 'Yesterday' coming to him in a dream. Keith Richard wrote the riff for '(I Can't Get No) Satisfaction' in his sleep. And 'Norwegian Wood' came to John Lennon in the same way.

"I'd spent five hours that morning trying to write a song that was meaningful and good," Lennon recalled, "and I finally gave up and lay down. Then, 'Nowhere Man' came, words and music, the whole damn thing. You try to go to sleep, but the song won't let you. So you have to get up and make it into something...."

More recently, The Smiths' Johnny Marr said: "I sleep in little three or four hour bursts and then I get these creative ideas around three o'clock in the morning. Sometimes I go to bed late and then wake up two hours later and I've got a better song."

# # # #

#26
MAKING YOUR SONG TOO PERSONAL

"I write songs that make people feel and that touch people"
—Janis Ian

THE BIGGEST mistake that many new songwriters make is to write songs that are all about them, their life, and their world. Who cares?

By all means express yourself by writing about something you're familiar with, but don't be too insular. Always remember that your songs should be about your audience—not about you.

If you want your songs to be successful commercially (which is all that music publishers and A&R executives are interested in) you must be careful not to make your songs too narrow and personal. The same applies whether you're a singer-songwriter, or writing for your own band or other artists.

Don't be like the boring person at a party who only ever wants to talk about himself or herself. People don't want to hear about your problems. They might, however, want to listen if your songs are about experiences, hardships and situations that everyone can relate to—such as a broken love affair, a personal tragedy, or a song about concern for the environment.

"I'm not looking to describe something that's only true of my own circumstances," Jackson Browne once said. "It's all about reaching inside to something that you have in common with many."

Diane Warren avoids making her songs too personal by putting herself in the shoes of the character she's writing about. "I see pictures in my mind and become the character in the song as I'm writing," she said. "It's kind of method songwriting, where you're the actor in the song."

By writing about something that everyone experiences in his or her own life, you can touch people's emotions. If you can make the listener feel something, it's the sign of a good song.

#27
BEING TOO SELF-INDULGENT

"Sometimes I'll do something clever, but I try not to be clever just to be clever—that would be contrived"
—Stephen Stills

UNLESS YOU'RE simply writing to please yourself or entertain your family, it is essential to take the listener and the commercial market into consideration when creating your songs. Don't just write for yourself.

As Emeli Sandé puts it: "You need to understand the market you're in. You can't become too self-indulgent."

The urge to express yourself may be one reason why you started writing in the first place—especially if you're a singer-songwriter or writing for your own band. However, there is a huge difference between communicating your personal thoughts and feelings forcefully in a song that has a well-balanced shape and form ... and an introspective self-indulgent opus that goes on and on, doesn't actually go anywhere, and only gratifies your own whims.

If you want your songs to be heard and enjoyed by other people, you have to be able to step outside of yourself and hear the song from the listener's point of view.

Does your song communicate clearly what you want to say without it needing further explanation? Are there chord changes and musical phrases that are repeated more than three times within a verse or a chorus just because you like them?

Have you written too many verses when, with some self-discipline, your story could be condensed and told in two or three high-impact verses?

Is your bridge too long and meandering? Are you deliberately trying to be obtuse and abstract to make your lyrics sound 'intellectual'?

If you want to be able to earn a living from songwriting, you're unlikely to achieve substantial commercial success by writing self-centered and self-satisfying songs that don't engage listeners and therefore fail to communicate your messages easily to them.

# # # #

#28
MAKING YOUR SONG TOO COMPLICATED

"Anytime I write something that's trying to be too smart, it doesn't work."
—Emeli Sandé

MOST SONGS tend to be between three and five minutes long, so you only have a limited amount of time in which to create a lasting impression—whether the listener is a music publisher, an A&R rep, a record producer, or a potential record buyer.

If your song structure and lyrics are too complicated, the song could end up sounding clumsy and difficult to understand—and listeners may find it hard to grasp what you're trying to communicate to them.

Don't fall into the trap of believing that you have to make every line clever or tricky in order to demonstrate your talent and originality.

Just make sure your song form is clear, predictable and easy to follow. Keeping it simple will make it easier for people to remember the song.

Listeners have subconsciously come to expect to hear certain elements in today's songs. That's why the four tried and tested variations of the Verse, Chorus, Verse, Chorus, Bridge, Chorus form are used again and again by top writers.

Even an intense writer like Laura Nyro revealed that she had a love for basic song structure. "Although sometimes you'd never know it," she admitted.

Don't make your chord progressions so complicated that they don't flow properly and end up wandering aimlessly. Having said that, you don't have to make them too predictable. Throw in a few surprise chords from time to time to keep the song interesting.

Carefully analyze your songs to make sure you're not putting too many messages into them. Remember, a song should contain only one story or one message told from a single point of view. Lyrically, you can avoid confusion by using the viewpoint character's thoughts and perceptions to drive the song.

These days, many pop singles are 'produced' rather than 'written' in the traditional sense. They rely on stacks of instrumentation and vocals and clever studio techniques. But a great song is one that still works and has an emotional impact on an audience when it is stripped down to just one vocal and a single guitar or piano. Think Adele … a piano … and 'Someone Like You'.

As Sting once remarked: "Songs have to be simple. It's not like you have a huge canvas to paint on or a novel length to fill. You've got to tell the story in two verses, a chorus and a coda and that takes some skill."

# # # #

#29
MAKING YOUR SECTIONS TOO LONG … OR TOO SHORT

MANY NEW songwriters often end up with individual sections in their songs that are either way too long, much too short, or not the same length each time they are used.

Such an imbalance in the structure of a song can make it sound clumsy and difficult to understand.

The song may also lack the essential symmetry that gives listeners a reassuring sense of predictability which can subconsciously influence their opinion of a song.

The best way to develop a good understanding of the ideal length for each building block in today's hit songs is by analyzing these individual sections yourself, by ear. Take your favorite songs apart, see how they are constructed, and time the length of each intro, verse, pre-chorus, chorus and bridge.

INTRO

You are likely to find that an intro is typically between 10-14 seconds long (4-8 bars) and the first verse is usually reached within 15 seconds. Intros for ballads tend to be shorter in order to get the listener into the body of the song faster.

VERSE

Most verses last for about 45 seconds, on average, and are usually eight bars long (although some may have 12 bars or 16 bars).

PRE-CHORUS

If a pre-chorus is used, it is often two or four bars in length (about 5-10 seconds)—with the verse correspondingly shorter to allow the song to hit the first chorus within 60 seconds.

CHORUS

Most choruses are often four bars or eight bars long (about 30 seconds).

BRIDGE

The bridge is frequently about 30 seconds long, about the same length as the chorus.

The overall length of your song is also important because listeners may lose interest if it is too long (because they think it's boring) or too short (because they feel it lacks substance and they don't find it satisfying).

#30
GETTING THE LENGTH OF YOUR SONG WRONG

THE HUGE importance of gaining radio airplay in order to secure a hit single means you have to make sure your song is an acceptable length for radio programmers. It should not be too long, or too short.

These days, the optimum length for a pop song is probably around three minutes 45 seconds.

In the 1950s and early 1960s, all hit songs were under three minutes long—chiefly because 10-inch 78rpm discs and the early 7-inch 45rpm vinyl singles were limited to about three minutes per side (some classic rock hits from the Fifties and Sixties are barely two minutes long!).

Since the early 1970s, though, song length has not been limited by recording technology. It is radio that has been calling the shots. That's why the average length of a hit song hasn't really changed much for nearly five decades.

Radio stations still tend to prefer singles that are between 2½ to 3½ minutes long (including the intro) because they believe that's what their listeners want.

And if it takes more than a minute for listeners to hear the title line and hook for the first time, you'll have to find a way to get there faster.

There are always exceptions of course. Queen's 'Bohemian Rhapsody' runs for five minutes 55 seconds (and doesn't even have a chorus)—and Don McLean's 'American Pie' is eight minutes 33 seconds long, although radio stations usually play the heavily edited four minutes 11 seconds version.

To get an idea of how long your finished song is likely to be, try timing it as soon as you've written a verse and a chorus. These days, the running time for most hit singles includes two verses, a bridge and a chorus that appears at least four times during the song.

If the song is likely to be under three minutes long, you should try to find a way of extending it—perhaps by adding a bridge, or by using an existing bridge twice. This can typically add an extra 20-30 seconds to a song.

You can gain a similar amount of additional time by inserting a third verse or an extra chorus. If you decide to add another chorus, try putting the additional chorus in a higher key to give your song an extra lift. A key change at the end of the song will prevent the final chorus repeats from becoming boring.

If your sole objective is to get your song picked up by a music publisher, A&R department or a record producer, don't pad the song out unnecessarily—for example, by throwing in a long guitar solo. Similarly, a two-minute intro or an extended instrumental outro may test the listener's patience … and certainly won't help you sell the song.

# # # #

#31
YOU'RE BORING US… GET TO THE CHORUS

"You don't want to hear a song on the radio that takes a long time before getting to the point"
—Robin Gibb

A COMMON mistake made by many aspiring songwriters is to cram so much into a verse that it becomes way too long—and delays the arrival of the all-important melodic 'hook' and title line in the chorus.

After all, the chorus is the part of the song that is meant to get stuck in people's heads. It is the section that really sells your song. So it's important to make sure that a strong dynamic flow in the verse transports the listener to an emotional lift in the first chorus as quickly as possible.

A lot depends on the tempo of your song, of course, but an analysis of today's hit songs shows us that you should ideally aim to arrive at the chorus around 30-45 seconds into the song—and certainly not later than 60 seconds.

There is a danger that an overly-long verse will bore listeners, and they may lose interest if they're expected to sit through the intro and at least one complete verse before arriving at what is meant to be the most memorable moment in the song.

On the other hand, the time it takes to reach the chorus ceases to be a problem if you start the song with the chorus … and then go into the first verse!

When asked to describe the ideal structure of a hit song, Foo Fighters' Dave Grohl once quipped: "It's chorus, chorus, pre-chorus, chorus, verse kinda, chorus, pre-chorus, chorus, chorus, chorus … In other words, don't bore us, get to the chorus."

# # # #

#32
NOT USING THE VERSE AS A STEPPING STONE

"There is a skill in getting to the heart of the song and not letting it get too long before getting to that feeling"
—Robin Gibb

THE PRIMARY role of the verse is to tell the song's story like a chapter in a book, with different words and new information in each verse to drive the story forward.

But songwriters who are just starting out often don't realize that the verse has another extremely important, strategic function.

It is also the stepping stone to the chorus.

The verses should be used to engage listeners' minds and take them step by step through your story—with the first verse introducing and establishing the overall concept of the song.

At the same time, each verse should build melodically toward the chorus and the all-important hook in the title line.

If your verse doesn't do this effectively, it isn't doing its job.

As previously mentioned in this book, most of today's hit songs are written in the verse-chorus form using one of five well-established structures:

1. Verse, Chorus, Verse, Chorus, Verse, Chorus.
2. Verse, Chorus, Verse, Chorus, Bridge, Chorus.
3. Chorus, Verse, Chorus, Verse, Chorus.
4. Verse, Verse, Chorus, Verse, Chorus, Chorus.
5. Verse, Pre-Chorus, Chorus, Verse, Pre-Chorus, Chorus.

As you can see, the verse is the gateway to the chorus in each case. You need to carefully plan what you want to say in each verse and then create a melodic and lyrical pathway that sustains and builds the listener's interest without delaying the chorus.

That's why many top writers' creative focus is on short lyrical imagery in their verses rather than using long explanations to tell the story. Remember, you need to reach the 'pay-off' in the chorus within 45-60 seconds.

As Robin Gibb of The Bee Gees once observed: "If you have a verse which goes on too long without getting to the emotional high of the song then you might be defeating the object.

"You don't want to hear a song on the radio that takes a long time before getting to the point."

# # # #

#33
NOT MAKING YOUR SONG STAND OUT

AS A publisher, I've heard countless songs by new writers that sounded pretty good, but I still passed on them because they lacked that something extra that makes a song stand out as a potential hit.

In many cases, the absence of that 'special something' was down to the writers not paying enough attention to the dynamics within their songs.

The writers may have come up with an interesting title, a nice melody and good lyrics, but they made their song weaker by not making full use of techniques such as contrast, tension and variation—all key elements in the craft of successful songwriting.

The effective use of contrast is all about making each section of your song sound different from the other segments. These differences hold listeners' attention and help them to distinguish between the verse, chorus and bridge. The changes also enable you to surprise listeners and stimulate their interest at crucial points in the song.

Try analyzing some current hit songs and you'll hear how the writers have increased the impact of their songs by using contrast and tension to make certain sections stand out.

The simplest way to add contrast, and keep your song sounding fresh, is by making sure the melody line (and chord progression) in the chorus is different from the verse ... and different again in the bridge.

It is essential for the chorus—and its all-important melodic hook—to stand out from the rest of the song to make it memorable, and so increase the song's commercial potential.

This can be achieved by starting the chorus melody higher than the last note of the verse—or even in a higher key—to set it apart.

A chorus rhyming pattern that is different from the verse will add extra contrast, as will a change in the rhythm of the words—such as a shift from staccato lyrics in the verse to stretched-out words in the chorus (or vice-versa).

Tension is another element that can give a song extra character.

You can build tension melodically within the verse by starting on lower notes and then making the melody climb higher and higher as the verse unfolds—before releasing the tension in the chorus. Tension can also be created lyrically by building up the song's story—perhaps changing the lyric meter from line-to-line as the verse progresses—until you reach your punchline (usually the title) in the chorus.

Unless you find that 'special something' to make your song stand out, there is always a danger that you'll have a boring song that stays on one level and sounds the same all the way through—like a damp firework that burns half-heartedly for three minutes but never ignites enough to display its true beauty.

# # # #

#34
FAILING TO MAKE AN EMOTIONAL CONNECTION

"Feelings are stronger than ideas or words in a song. You can have a thousand ideas, but unless you capture an emotion, it's an essay"
—Bono

FOR A song to become a great song, it must be able to reach out and touch listeners and stimulate an emotional response within them. It should make them feel something.

It should take them on a memorable and emotional journey.

Unfortunately, many new writers fail to take full advantage of music's unique ability to evoke and express a wide range of emotions – from sadness and the pain of a lost love … to joy, and the urge to get up and dance.

The Bee Gees' Robin Gibb always believed that emotion should be the bedrock of any song. "Putting melody and emotion together can create something magical," he once remarked. "There is something very appealing to all ages when you are singing about human emotions. Emotions will reach out over the decades."

He added: "Always look for new and alternative ways to sing about human emotions and show them in a different light that people haven't heard before."

There is no single formula for achieving an emotional connection with the listener, but all the ingredients are there in your melodies, lyrics, chord progressions, tempos and rhythms.

You have to combine these elements to build a dynamic structure that contains underlying patterns of unresolved tension – perhaps by using minor chords or a dominant chord (e.g. G in the key of C) that doesn't return to the 'home' chord (C in the key of C) until the tension is released. Major chords often convey happiness or joy, while minor chords are associated with sadness. Using a mix of minor chords and major chords can add extra depth and color to a song.

The great George Gershwin once described songwriting as "an emotional science", and scientific studies have shown that a wide range of notes can imply joy or uneasiness, while a narrower range of notes can suggest tranquility, sadness or triumph.

Consonant or complementing harmonies are connected with feelings of happiness and relaxation, while dissonant or clashing harmonies tend to imply excitement or anger.

Studies have also confirmed the long-recognized association between up-tempo songs and feelings of happiness or excitement, and a slow tempo with a sense of romance or sadness.

If you are moved emotionally by your melody or lyrics—or the combination of both—then your song may also connect with other people, and that's what you need to achieve.

As Robbie Robertson once explained: "I got into music in the very beginning because I heard music that gave me chills. And I thought, 'I want to do that. I want to give somebody else chills!' So, for me, it's all about discovering the emotions in the music."

Elton John takes a similar view. "If you write great songs with meaning and emotion, they will last for ever because songs are the key to everything," he said. "They will outlast the artist."

Try testing your completed song on the people closest to you, someone who will give you an honest opinion. If the song doesn't genuinely move them in its rawest, stripped-down form—one vocal and a single guitar or piano—the song has failed.

Don't fool yourself into thinking a magical transformation will take place in the studio if you decide to spend money on making a demo of the song. Trying to create an emotional connection with the aid of lots of production frills won't fool a music publisher or an A&R rep. They always look to the song inside the recording.

As Neil Sedaka once observed: "The most challenging task for a songwriter is to write a simple tune but still bring an emotional feeling to it ... No frills. No production gimmicks."

# # # #

#35
BEING TOO PREDICTABLE

NEW WRITERS often don't realize that striking a good balance between predictability and surprise is one of the most important characteristics of a hit song.

Whilst your song should have a familiar structure so that it feels right to listeners and helps to retain their interest, it should not be too predictable.

If what's going to happen next in your song is too obvious, listeners may get bored and switch off. However, if the song is too different or too complex, they won't feel comfortable and may still tune out.

Music publishers and A&R executives always say they're looking for new material that is inventive and original—yet they're often reluctant to sign songs that are totally unlike anything they've ever heard before. At the end of the day, what they really want is something that sounds different, but is still familiar enough to be played by mainstream radio stations.

That's why your song needs to sound familiar ... but not similar.

A sense of predictability in your chord progressions, melodies or rhyming patterns can be reassuring and a source of comfort for listeners. At the same time, though, your song still has to stand out from all the other music tracks that people are likely to hear on the radio or online.

The answer is to include a few surprises—such as a twist in your lyrics ... an unexpected chord change or key change ... or a chord change that listeners expect to hear, but don't.

For example, dominant chords (those built on the fifth note in the scale) naturally want to move to the tonic chord (the 'home' note in the scale). By playing the dominant chord (e.g. G or G7 in the key of C), you can make listeners believe the 'home' chord (C in the key of C) is about to follow ... but, instead, you can surprise the listener by deliberately moving to a completely different chord. This can help to build energy and tension in the song.

Roger Nichols, who wrote The Carpenters' 'We've Only Just Begun' and Three Dog Night's 'Out In the Country' with Paul Williams, likes to build a surprise into his bridge sections: "If you can surprise the listener then that bridge is going to stay with him longer," he says, "and it won't just be a point in the song when the listener's ear is vamping waiting to get back to the song's main melody."

# # # #

#36
NOT GIVING YOUR SONG A KILLER HIGH POINT

"You must find an emotional moment in a song. A film can only go for about seven minutes before it must have an emotional moment on the screen. With songs it's the same, except you have three minutes—not 90 minutes—to make everything happen"
—Ray Davies

NEW SONGWRITERS often tend to overlook the importance of building a melodic 'high point' into their songs. This powerful climactic moment is usually the result of several elements of the song coming together at the same time—producing an emotional high that provides an important focal point for the listener.

This special moment causes an increase in momentum, tension and intensity which, in turn, creates a sense of excitement that helps to make the song more memorable to the listener.

Finding the ideal location for a song's melodic high point is an important part of the craft of songwriting. There is no golden rule, only that it should ideally happen closer to the end of the song—typically in the final third—so that the song can build up to it

That's why the melodic peak is usually heard in the chorus rather than in the verse—although verses can also have an explosion of emotion (as long as the climax in the chorus is higher up the scale than in the verse).

Many established writers place the climactic moment in the second half of their chorus, often on the third line of a four-line chorus. It can coincide with the song's title, or be placed just before the title line at the end of the chorus.

Other writers position a special high point just before the last chorus, sometimes in the bridge.

"There is a basic part of the song that flowers and you can hear it," said the Bee Gees' Robin Gibb. "I don't think a lot of new songwriters are getting to grips with it. Knowing where the flowering is, where the song blossoms, where the emotional highs and lows of the song should be is so important."

He added: "There is a skill in getting to the heart of the song and not letting it get too long before getting to that feeling."

# # # #

#37
TOO MANY IDEAS IN YOUR SONG

"Songs are life in 80 words or less"
—Neil Diamond

WRITERS WHO are just starting out often feel they have to cram as much as possible into a song in order to impress music publishers, A&R reps or record producers. But if you really want your song to pack a punch, you should concentrate on just one strong message or emotion …and build your song around it.

After coming up with a first verse and chorus, you may feel compelled to move on to a different topic in the second verse, and maybe another new theme in the bridge. But, far from impressing people, presenting multiple ideas in this way can have the opposite effect.

Your song should make one major point, from one point of view.

If you try to explore too many ideas or themes, there is a danger that you will send out mixed messages to the listener. The last thing you want is to confuse people so much that they end up losing interest in your song.

That's why many established songwriters believe simplicity is an important common denominator in all successful songs.

Don't say more than you need to, and say what you need to say concisely and clearly.

To prevent your song from going off in too many directions, you need to be clear about the whole point of the song before you start writing. You should be able to describe what the song is about in one short phrase.

According to Jimmy Webb, clarity is "the single greatest shortcoming" of new songwriters and their work. "If a young songwriter doesn't really know what he wants to say, how the hell is he going to say it?" says Webb. "That's why I tell a lot of songwriters to start with titles."

Some pro writers find it helpful to sketch out the complete storyline for a song in a few paragraphs of prose, like a mini-treatment for a movie or a novel. If you take this approach, the next step is to add rhymes to your prose and turn the words used in your 'treatment' into the song's lyrics. You then have to match the phrasing patterns with the melody and the number of beats in each line.

After you've written the first verse, subsequent verses and the bridge should go deeper into the storyline—just like a tale unfolding in each new chapter of a novel. Unlike a novel, though, you only have about three minutes and a limited number of words to really explore your theme.

"If you have a clear idea of what you want to say," Lyle Lovett observed, "then you know when you have said it, and the song is finished."

# # # #

#38
LACK OF FOCUS

"When your song is called 'XYZ' or whatever, every line has got to make sense against your title"
—Merle Haggard

I KNOW from personal experience that there is nothing more frustrating for a music publisher than taking the time to listen to a demo by a new writer and then finding that the song just wanders aimlessly with no apparent direction. The irritation that this causes often results in even the most generous publisher hitting the 'stop' button after about 30 seconds.

A lack of focus is one of the biggest weaknesses of many aspiring writers' songs. This is usually because the writer has no idea where the song is heading when he or she starts working on it. As a result, the song simply meanders from one chord to the next without any purpose and with no clear distinction between different sections.

A clear focus is also a critical aspect of effective lyric writing. Can you express the subject of your song in a single phrase? Even if the song is not meant to follow a linear storyline, the overall song won't have a cohesive feel to it if you don't focus on one subject and develop this theme as the song progresses.

To make sure your lyrics are focused, start with a strong title and then try asking yourself Who? What? Where? When? How? and Why?-type questions prompted by the title.

A title like 'Heartbreak Sunrise', for example, would suggest questions such as "What is happening at sunrise?", "Who's going to be heartbroken?", "Why are they going to be heartbroken?". The answers to these questions will generate words, phrases and images that are relevant to the overall theme and can be used in the lyrics.

If your song is simply allowed to 'evolve' without any shape or direction, there is a danger that listeners will become completely lost and may lose interest. So don't just go with the first thing that comes into your head. Set out a clear 'road map' for the song.

Once you know where you want to get to, you need to plan your route carefully so that your chord progression reaches your destination—the all-important melodic hook and title line in the chorus—as quickly as possible.

As Jimmy Webb once said: "I usually know what kind of song I'm after. I know what I'm trying to do when I start. I don't always get there. But I try to visualize what it's actually going to be."

# # # #

PART 3:

COMPONENTS OF A HIT SONG

#39
TITLES THAT DON'T HELP YOU SELL THE SONG

"I write from titles. I don't write the first line of a song. It's a mistake, because then you have to come up with the second one"
—Sting

ACCORDING TO some estimates, more than one million new songs are released every year. That's an awful lot of songs for you to compete with!

But you have a powerful weapon that can help you stand out from the crowd ... YOUR SONG TITLE. A great title can be your song's strongest selling point and the best way to attract the attention of listeners and buyers.

To make an impact, though, it is essential for the title to be unique and distinctive—and easy to remember. It must be able to tell people what the song is about in just one word or a single phrase, and in not more than seven syllables.

Intriguing and attention-grabbing titles are also essential to make your songs stand out when you submit demos to music publishers and A&R reps. They receive hundreds of new songs every week, but an interesting title can go a long way toward helping your song get into their 'must-listen-to' pile.

As Morrissey once remarked: "The title is often more important than the song because more people will read the title than hear the song, and the title will draw them in or repel them..."

The title has to be the emotional foundation of your song. So don't start writing until you have a title that moves you. If you're not inspired by the title, then it's unlikely that it will be able to achieve an emotional connection with listeners in order to sell your song.

So what makes a great title?

Experienced songwriters say short phrases or powerful single words work best. In fact, Foo Fighters' Dave Grohl reckons writers should treat their song titles like bumper stickers. His advice is: "Keep them simple, catchy and straight to the point".

Using action words in titles can attract attention and convey a strong image. And great ideas can come from newspaper headlines containing attention-grabbing phrases that people can relate to (after all, that's what newspaper headlines are there for).

Ideas for good titles can come from anything and everything around you. So always be prepared. Carry a notebook or use the voice memo option on your phone to capture exceptional ideas when you spot them. And make sure you keep a titles list. Never let a great title get away!

# # # #

#40
NOT POSITIONING THE TITLE CORRECTLY

AS WELL as giving your song an intriguing and attention-grabbing title, it is also vital to place the title line in the strongest possible position within the song. This is another aspect of the craft of songwriting that many new writers overlook.

Easy recognition of the title is an important commercial consideration. It means record buyers who hear the song on the radio (or maybe during a scene from a TV drama series) will know what to look for online or at the record store.

Putting the title in the right place will make it much easier for people to recognize it and remember it. If the title is buried somewhere in the middle of the song, listeners may not be able to pick it out.

Trying humming your song without any lyrics and see how the melody leads you to a particular point where it feels natural to insert the title. This is most likely to be in the hardest-hitting part of your melody line: THE HOOK.

If you're using a Verse-Chorus structure, the most effective position is the first line or the last line (or both) of your chorus. This will allow the title to be repeated several times throughout the song like a catchphrase.

With the Verse-Verse-Bridge-Verse format, the title should either be in the first line or the last line of the verse. One of the most famous examples of this is Paul McCartney's 'Yesterday'

While it is generally accepted that the title has to be mentioned somewhere in a song, there are exceptions, of course.

'Unchained Melody' famously became one of the most recorded songs of all time despite not having the title in the lyrics. However, its backstory is a little different from most hit songs. Composer Alex North was originally asked to write the song as the theme for a 1955 prison movie called *Unchained*. As a result, it became known as "the Unchained melody". When lyricist Hy Zaret came to add the words, he decided to focus the story on a prisoner who is pining for a lover he hasn't seen in a "long, lonely time". And the word 'unchained' is not mentioned once!

At the other end of the scale, in Rihanna's 2012 hit single 'Diamonds'—written by Sia Furler and producers Benny Blanco and StarGate—the title is sung 35 times in three minutes and 45 seconds!

# # # #

#41
FORGETTING THE TUNE'S THE THING

"It's the lyric that makes a song a hit, but the tune is what makes it last"
—Irving Berlin

NO MATTER which music genre you're writing for—whether it's pop, rock, country, R&B or any other style—the melody line is second only to the title as the most important part of a song.

The melody is the first thing that listeners catch when they hear a song for the first time. If they like the tune, they're more likely to want to start listening to the words. That's why melodies need good hooks, and why a strong and memorable melody is the chief reason why most songs become hits.

It is also important to make sure that the melody in your chorus is significantly different from the verse melody to make it stand out. In most hit songs, the chorus melody is usually placed higher in the scale—or in a higher key—than the last note of the verse.

A weak melody can't be fixed in the recording studio with the aid of lots of production gimmicks. People won't be able to hum vocal effects, drum fills or instrumental breaks.

"If you have a keyboard that's MIDI'd with a couple of synthesizers, so you have strings and horns, you can sound glorious," said Burt Bacharach. "But when you take it all apart, when you peel back the cover, what do you have? Do you really have a song, do you really have a melody?"

According to Glenn Frey, The Eagles put such a strong emphasis on writing memorable melodies that they even try to make their guitar solos 'sing-able'.

Robin Gibb once explained that the Bee Gees always made sure they had a great melody before they started writing the lyrics. "The principle is to let the melody dictate the flow of the lyrics," he said. "A good melody is not something you should labor at. It should come easily. If you can't remember it, then it's probably not worth it."

He added: "If the melody doesn't get you off, the chances are it won't get other people off either."

# # # #

#42
MAKING YOUR MELODY HARD TO REMEMBER

"Never be ashamed to write a melody that people remember"
—Burt Bacharach

NEW SONGWRITERS often feel they have to come up with clever, intricate melodies in order to show how talented and 'original' they are. But publishing companies and record labels are commercial organizations that need to make money. They're really only interested in one thing: songs that can potentially sell millions of records and downloads around the world.

Creating songs with strong commercial appeal is all about achieving a unique blend of originality, familiarity and predictability that will make a song as easy to remember as possible.

Because people listen to the words and the music at the same time, it is especially important to retain simplicity in the melody. As Emeli Sandé puts it: "Sometimes simple melodies have the greatest impact."

But that's where new writers often go wrong. They worry that their songs will be regarded as boring, simplistic and unworthy if they don't compose elaborate melodies. As a result, they can end up with songs that are far too complicated.

If people can't hum or whistle your song after a few listens, it is unlikely to be a commercial success.

Many experienced writers find that simple tunes can be just as hard to write as a complex piece. "Writing a simple melody can take weeks to get it right where I want it," admits former Yes guitarist Trevor Rabin.

If you take time to analyze some of today's biggest hit songs, you'll find that it is their simplicity that makes them so memorable. They are almost always built on just two or three short melodic themes that link together to form bigger lines. Simple phrases containing between two and seven notes are much easier to remember after one listen. And when these short phrases are combined and repeated several times throughout the song, they can deliver a powerful and memorable melody.

Listen to the choruses of some of the biggest-selling songs of the past 50 years—songs that have stood the test of time. You will hear that most of them have a short, catchy melodic hook that is also usually the title line. The hook features a melody and lyrics that are exactly the same every time the chorus is repeated—thus making sure the song gets well and truly stuck in the listener's head!

It is this repetition of musical phrases that helps to make each song sound simple, even if it isn't. And, as the great Irving Berlin once remarked, it helps the melody to "linger" in the listener's head long after the song has ended.

# # # #

#43
YOUR MELODY AND LYRICS AREN'T COMPATIBLE

"When I hear music I hear words, just as I assume the composer hears music when he listens to lyrics"
—Hal David

YOUR SUCCESS as a hit songwriter depends on your ability to communicate stories, feelings and messages that reach out and touch listeners and evoke an emotional response within them (whether it's an urge to get up and dance ... or to get all romantic).

The key to achieving this lies in the compatibility of your words and music.

Your melody is the powerful medium through which your lyrical content is delivered to the listener. The melody helps to interpret the emotional intensity of the lyrics, and also helps people to remember the words.

It is therefore vital to make sure the melody and lyrics complement each other perfectly in order to convey the essence and meaning of your song. You have to make sure your words and melody belong together.

The technique known as prosody—the way in which words and syllables line up with the notes in the melody line—is a valuable device for making it easier to communicate exactly what you're trying to say in your song. For example, aligning downbeats or accented notes with stressed syllables or key words can play a powerful role in conveying meaning.

Music has a unique ability to express and elicit a wide range of emotions to match the accompanying lyrics. Major chords can convey happiness or joy, while minor chords create a feeling of melancholy or sadness. You can use a mix of minor chords, major chords and the tension created by unresolved chords to match what you're saying in each line of your lyrics.

It all comes down to experimenting with chords, intervals, rhythms and phrasing patterns to find the most effective way of marrying your melody and lyrics. When you find a combination that really moves you, it's likely to move other people too.

# # # #

#44
YOUR MELODY RANGE IS TOO WIDE

IF YOU'RE a singer-songwriter—or if you write for your own band—your melodies will naturally be tailored to fit your own vocal range or that of your band's lead singer. But if your aim is to get other artists to record your songs, it is important to make sure your melody lines don't exceed the vocal range of the intended singers.

For example, if you have to break into falsetto when you sing the song yourself, it's a sign that the melody range may be too wide.

A singer's vocal range is often defined as the total span of "musically useful" pitches that he or she can produce. In other words, if the lowest notes are barely audible when the artist sings them, and the highest notes crack and can't be sustained, then they aren't "musically useful".

The maximum range for most singers is rarely more than one and a half octaves (in many cases it's an octave plus a couple of notes). So if your song has a much greater melodic span than that, you may be limiting the number of artists who could sing the song comfortably.

Remember, successful artists who don't write their own material are constantly being bombarded with new songs. Because they have so many to choose from, they're unlikely to go for a song that they find difficult to sing (especially live)—no matter how much they like it.

# # # #

#45
"TOO MANY NOTES, MOZART"

WHEN EMPEROR Joseph II first heard Wolfgang Amadeus Mozart's opera *The Abduction from the Seraglio* in 1782, he famously told the composer: "Too many notes, my dear Mozart".

It was a criticism shared by many people at the time—even amongst Mozart's admirers. He had such a fertile melodic mind, and his head was so full of catchy tunes, that he could not resist cramming them all into his music.

Today, new writers often make the same mistake. Their tunes may not be in the same league as Mozart, of course, but they try to squeeze too much into their melodies in order to demonstrate their talent and impress people.

Too many notes can be a problem if you want other artists to be able to sing your songs. So be careful not to make your melodies so busy that there are no resting spaces or pauses in which the poor singer can draw a breath!

For singers, good breath management skills are essential if they want to sound great and maintain the quality of their vocal performance every time. If you don't allow the singer enough space to breathe, it can have a negative impact on his or her vocal quality—and the song may be rejected as a result.

It is important to structure the musical phrases in your song in such a way that the singer can take a breath without it sounding awkward—like breathing naturally between sentences when you're talking. Notes held for more than a few beats should ideally be followed by a rest long enough to allow a breath. You should also leave some breathing space after a string of fast, short notes.

It is also essential to leave enough spaces (lyrically and melodically) to allow artists to express themselves and interpret the song in their own way.

The best way to check the 'breathability' of your song is to print out the lyrics, read them out loud against a metronome or a click track, and mark all of the points at which you find yourself taking a breath in normal speech. Then make sure the notes you're asking the vocalist to sing correspond with these natural pauses.

Many experienced songwriters believe it is the gaps and pauses left between the notes that actually help to make the overall melody sound interesting and catchy.

# # # #

#46
TOO MUCH REPETITION (OR TOO LITTLE)

ONE OF the most significant features of today's hit songs is the heavy use of repetition. Certain musical themes and lyrics are deliberately repeated throughout the song to make it sound instantly 'familiar' and therefore much easier for listeners to remember.

This is especially important when relying on radio airplay to help 'break' a new single. Most songs require multiple radio plays over several weeks in order to climb the charts, so repetition of key melodic phrases and lyrics (especially the title line in the chorus) is a powerful way to firmly plant the song in listeners' heads.

Studies have found that people often feel more comfortable listening to a song they already know, or when they hear a new song that sounds kind of familiar and predictable.

But new songwriters often struggle when it comes to finding the right balance between repeating musical phrases often enough to make the song memorable … and using too much repetition which can make the song sound insignificant, twee and boring.

Too little repetition and you can't hold listeners' attention; too much repetition and you turn them off; and no repetition at all can make your melody sound far too complicated to be remembered easily.

That's why your songs need to have a good balance of predictability (through repetition) and surprise … without overdoing one or the other.

To find out how successful writers manage to achieve this, take time to analyze some of today's biggest hit songs. Pick out the melodic themes, riffs and lyrics that you hear again and again. The repeated sections may comprise only a few notes or they could be several bars long. Many songs typically feature about 10 repetitions of the title throughout the song.

Make a note of how and where the repeated sections are used in each song—and apply a similar technique to your own songs.

# # # #

#47
YOUR REPEATED SECTIONS AREN'T CONSISTENT

AS MENTIONED previously, a prominent feature of many of today's hit songs is the frequent repetition of key melodic phrases.

Certain musical themes and lyrics (especially the 'hook' and title line) are deliberately repeated throughout the song to make it sound instantly familiar to listeners, and therefore much easier to remember.

While new writers may understand the importance of establishing melodic hooks, some of them fail to grasp that 'repetition' means their verse melody has to be exactly the same in every verse, and their chorus and pre-chorus melodies should also be consistent throughout the song.

Repetition is a powerful way of firmly planting your song in listeners' heads, but if you include too many melody changes (no matter how subtle) from verse to verse and chorus to chorus, you will make it harder for listeners to remember them all so that they can easily sing along.

# # # #

#48
NO CONTRAST BETWEEN VERSE AND CHORUS

"Sometimes an unexpected chord change can be the difference between a good song and a great song"
—Gary Talley

YOU MAY only have one chance to get a music publisher or an A&R executive to listen to your song, so it is essential to make sure the chorus— which is the section that is supposed to really sell your song—stands out clearly when people hear it for the first time.

With songs by new, inexperienced writers, though, it is sometimes difficult to tell where the verse ends and the chorus begins. Writers who are just starting out often don't realize that a lack of contrast between the chorus and the verse weakens the overall song.

That's why it is essential for the chorus melody to be significantly different from the verse melody, with a different chord progression. The chorus should ideally start on a different chord from the first chord of the verse, perhaps using an unexpected chord change to surprise the listener.

Varying the rhythm of your verse melody and chorus melody will also help to create contrast. For example, if your verse consists of note lengths that are fairly short, try using long, sustained notes in the chorus melody (or vice versa).

Contrast can also be achieved by giving the verse melody a strong dynamic flow that leads the listener to an emotional 'lift' in the chorus—with the chorus melody typically placed higher in the scale than the last note of the verse.

You can also use your lyrics to add greater contrast by making the chorus rhyme scheme different from that of the verse.

A change in the rhythm of the words—such as a shift from staccato lyrics in the verse to stretched-out words in the chorus (or vice-versa) —will also help to provide a clear distinction between the two sections.

# # # #

#49
WHERE'S YOUR 'CALL TO ACTION'?

IN THE advertising business, they use a device called the 'call to action' to influence people's behavior and encourage consumers to do something such as "Buy now while stocks last!" or "Call this number now!" or "Like us on Facebook and get a free gift!".

In your song, the CHORUS is the 'call to action'.

It's the section that is meant to persuade people to listen to the rest of the song, and then go out and buy the record!

Publishers and A&R execs will look for this 'call to action' when they hear your song for the first time.

They want to be sure that, if the song gets played on radio, the chorus will stand out enough to attract the listener's attention when he or she is busy doing something else.

This means the chorus melody should be extremely catchy, memorable and significantly different from the verse and the bridge, with a different chord progression.

Changing the beat on which the chorus melody starts can have a subconscious impact on the listener—especially if the verse melody begins on the second beat of the measure (the 'two-beat') and the chorus starts hammering home the hook on the first beat (like Kylie Minogue's infectious 'Can't Get You Out of My Head', written by Cathy Dennis and Rob Davis).

Some experienced writers put the chorus in a higher key to set it apart from the rest of the song. Other writers use a four-bar pre-chorus to add a burst of extra energy at the end of the verse.

Building a climactic moment into the chorus (usually during the third phrase of a 4-phrase chorus melody) also serves as a kind of fuel that adds momentum and energy to the song, while at the same time providing a musical goal for the melody, chords and lyrics.

All of these techniques can suddenly elevate the melody and let people know they are now in the chorus. While a soaring chorus can deliver a sense of satisfaction and emotional fulfillment for the listener, the heavily repeated hook drives home the title line as the musical 'call to action'.

# # # #

#50
LACK OF BALANCE BETWEEN CHORDS AND MELODY

"Interesting chords will compel interesting melodies"
—Jimmy Webb

NEW WRITERS often tend to develop the melody line for their songs by stringing together a sequence of random chords, without trying to achieve a good balance between the individual chords and the emotional message of the song. This can sometimes result in a song that sounds confusing or boring.

Your choice of chords can bring character and color to your song and give it a sense of direction. So don't just use the first chord that comes to you (although it may eventually prove to be the right one). Instead, assess every individual chord to make sure it matches the emotion of the melody and the lyrics.

Understanding how chords like to move—and how different chords harmonize with certain notes—is a vital part of the craft of songwriting. Most chord progressions work to pinpoint the 'home' chord (e.g. C in the key of C) as the harmonic and melodic objective.

Every chord has a different emotional tone. Major chords can convey happiness, joy or a positive feeling; minor chords create a sense of melancholy or sadness; and tension can be increased by using unresolved chords (chords that want to return to the 'home' chord, but don't).

Roger Nichols believes in using different inversions of a chord, or trying the song in a different key, to add extra color or character to a melody. "After I've finished a melody I generally play it in two or three different keys to see if anything is happening chord-wise," said Nichols. "Many times I'll hear a new chord in a different key. I basically compose the melody line by singing the melody that occurs to me as I play the undercarriage on the piano or guitar."

Jimmy Webb—who wrote the best-selling book *Tunesmith: Inside The Art of Songwriting*—believes creating a strong melody is all about finding the right chords. "It's very hard to write a boring melody to an interesting chord sequence," he said.

It is also important to consider the frequency of chord changes in each section of your song because this too can affect the balance between chords and melody.

In many songs, chords tend to change every four to eight beats—typically on the first and third beat of every bar. A song may sound boring if the chords don't change often enough, but changes that are too frequent and complex can distract listeners. Switching chords too often in an up-tempo song, for example, can make it sound frantic—so the faster your song the less frequent the changes should be.

It is also important to avoid using the same chord patterns again and again in your songs, otherwise they will start sounding identical.

Chord progressions can't be copyrighted, so try something different by building your own melody around the chord sequences used in several of today's hit songs. A word of warning though: while the basic shape of your song can be similar to the hit, make sure you DON'T copy the original melody or lyrics … or you'll be guilty of plagiarism!

# # # #

#51
YOUR CHORDS HAVE NO DIRECTION

AS MENTIONED previously in this book, most listeners— whether they're music publishers, A&R reps or ordinary record buyers—have a subconscious desire for symmetry when listening to music. This musical symmetry creates a sense of predictability that is reassuring and comforting to the listener.

The harmonic progression in a song's chord structure is an important source of this musical symmetry. Listeners like it when the overall sense of rhythmic and harmonic direction is clear and easy to follow.

A chord progression is defined as a series of chord changes that should have the definite goal of establishing a tonality founded on a key, root or 'home' chord (e.g. C in the key of C). In other words, the chord progression works to pinpoint the home note and the home chord as the harmonic and melodic objective. It moves away from the home chord as the melody unfolds and eventually returns to it to complete the melodic circle.

Unfortunately, many new writers use chord progressions that don't have any sense of direction or harmonic goal.

The chords just wander aimlessly and don't flow properly, giving the impression that they aren't actually going anywhere. As a result, there's a danger that the song won't feel right to listeners … and they'll quickly lose interest.

A good harmonic progression in any key has three basic parts: the home chord (e.g. C in the key of C); destination chords such as the 'pre-dominant' (D, F, etc. in the key of C) or the 'ultimate harmonic' (E, A, etc. in the key of C). The dominant or 'turning' chord (e.g. G or G7 in the key of C) then completes the progression by returning to the home chord (C).

As you try to evoke different moods to match your lyrics, some of your destination chords can be less predictable and more ambitious—such as chords that don't necessarily exist within your chosen key. What is essential, though, is that you complete the musical journey by finding a sensible way of getting back to the home chord.

It is this return to the home chord that leaves the listener feeling subconsciously 'satisfied' because the progression has been harmonically resolved.

# # # #

#52
AVOIDING MINOR CHORDS A MAJOR MISTAKE

"How strange the change from major to minor…"
—Cole Porter ('Ev'ry Time We Say Goodbye')

SOME NEW writers deliberately avoid using minor chords because they believe that sticking to major chords will make their songs sound happier and more positive … and consequently make listeners feel good about what they're hearing.

But writers who completely ignore minor chords are not only missing out on being able to add greater depth and character to their songs, they're also going against one of the most significant songwriting trends of the past 50 years.

In 2012, an academic study revealed that the number of minor chord hits has actually doubled since 1965, and fewer hit songs are now being written in major chords.

Music psychologist Professor E Glenn Schellenberg and sociologist Professor Christian von Scheve evaluated more than 1,000 American Top 40 songs that charted between 1965 and 2012. Their study found that in the second half of the 1960s, about 85% of songs that reached the top of the charts were written in a major mode, but by the second half of the 2000s that figure had fallen to only 43.5%.

"Just as the lyrics of pop songs have become more self-referential and negative in recent decades, the music has also changed—it sounds sadder and emotionally more ambivalent," Schellenberg and von Scheve explained in their study.

They added: "Listeners of popular music today like emotionally complex pieces. The use of minor chords makes it possible to express a greater scale of emotions in a single piece of music."

Minor chords can substantially change the mood or feel of your song. And they can often help you to emphasize or dramatize the meaning of certain words or phrases in your lyrics.

In the 1920s, George Gershwin started enhancing Tin Pan Alley 'pop' songs by frequently moving between major and minor chords in the same song in order to convey an emotional shift.

Throughout the late 1950s and early 1960s, hundreds of rock 'n' roll hits were based on just three basic chord progressions. And only one of them actually included a minor chord (the classic C-Am-F-G in the key of C, or G-Em-C-D in the key of G). This progression was heavily used by almost all of the early R&B, Motown and Brill Building songwriters.

Then along came The Beatles. The innovative songs of John Lennon and Paul McCartney helped to introduce a greater number of minor chords to rock 'n' roll—resulting in some unforgettable Beatles tunes that were built on simple but unexpected chords which chromatically shifted between keys, or between major and minor.

So don't just write in a major key. You'll be missing out on an entire palette of emotions—and neglecting a highly effective means of making your songs sound far more interesting and edgy.

# # # #

#53
YOUR SONGS ALL SOUND THE SAME

NEW WRITERS sometimes strike gold and discover a songwriting 'formula' that really works for them. It could be the result of a particular chord progression—or the use of a specific climactic chord change or musical phrase—but it helps them to create a new kind of song that evokes the best response they've ever had from listeners.

It's a great feeling to find that you've finally made such an important breakthrough in your songwriting. Naturally, you will want to take advantage of this winning 'formula' to help you establish your own distinctive sound and style.

But be careful not to end up writing songs that are all built around the same few notes, chords and keys.

While each new song may sound great on its own, there is a danger that you could end up with a collection of songs that all sound alike—especially if you put them together on the same demo submission or a showcase album (or on your own website, YouTube channel or Soundcloud page).

So don't keep using the same progressions again and again. Create a few surprises by inserting new chords into your basic 'formula'. Or take the same chords and twist them around.

You may find that trying out the same chord progression in two or three different keys can lead to a completely new melody line. If you're a guitarist, try playing your successful 'formula' on a piano (or vice versa). You may find it sparks a whole new set of ideas.

You can also make similarly-constructed songs sound different by varying the rhythm of your melodies. In other words, vary the note lengths from song to song (and within songs) to create contrast. Using a different combination of sustained notes, shorter notes and staccato notes will make your songs stand apart from each other.

And don't open every song in the same way. If most of your tracks have a four-bar instrumental intro, try adding some variety by starting a song with the chorus instead.

# # # #

#54
DON'T BE ORDINARY, BE EXTRAORDINARY

"It's not just finding interesting chords, it's how you sequence them—like stringing together pearls on a string"
—Jimmy Webb

WRITERS WHO are just starting out often end up building all their songs around the same notes, chords and keys—especially when they discover chord patterns that seem to work for them, or which they really like. As mentioned in #53, this can result in a collection of songs that all sound the same.

So don't just use ordinary chords, be extra-ordinary. Keep each new song sounding fresh and different by creating plenty of variety in your chord progressions.

There are several ways you can use unexpected chords to bring different textures and colors to your songs without losing harmonic cohesion. For example, you can surprise listeners by changing key during parts of your song—weaving together closely related keys that have common chords.

You can also use 'pivot' chords which enable you to move from the original key to the destination key by way of a chord that both keys share (e.g. inserting an E minor chord to help you move from C to A).

Then there's 'parallel' key modulation which allows you to change the mode but maintain the same tonal center (for example, one section of your song may be in the key of E major and you then modulate to E minor).

Distant keys can also be reached sequentially through closely related keys by using 'chain modulation' (for example C to G and then to D).

You can also use variant chords to make a chord progression harmonically interesting by simply replacing the default chords at any of the seven harmonic scale positions in your song.

Adding sixths, sevenths, ninths or suspended chords can also bring different flavors to the basic chord. For example, the verse of The Who's 'Pinball Wizard' features a sequence of suspended fourth chords that resolve to their major counterparts.

Major seventh chords can be very evocative and are common in most styles of pop music. Examples of tonic major seventh chords in hit songs include Labelle's 'Lady Marmalade', Chic's 'Le Freak', 'One of These Nights' by The Eagles, Bread's 'Make It With You', 'You've Made Me So Very Happy' by Blood Sweat & Tears, and Chicago's 'Color My World'.

You can also enhance the feel of your song by using so-called 'jazz chords', such as thirds, fifths, sevenths, ninths, elevenths or thirteenths.

In the 1920s, the great George Gershwin reshaped popular music by taking jazz elements and certain harmonies and combining them with Tin Pan Alley pop in a way that hadn't been done before.

In the modern era, 'jazz chords' such as ninths, elevenths and thirteenths are featured prominently in songs like Billy Joel's 'Just the Way You Are', 'Ebony and Ivory' by Paul McCartney and Stevie Wonder, and Mariah Carey's 'Love Takes Time'.

Carole King's classic song 'I Feel the Earth Move' even uses elevenths in a minor key!

Paul McCartney's 'Yesterday'—one of the most covered songs of all time—is a great example of how to make a simple tune harmonically interesting. The song doesn't just feature ordinary majors, minors and sevenths; it also includes a mixture of fifths, thirds and seconds, and a couple of well-chosen variant chords. The progression in the verse is: F-Em7-A7-Dm-Bflat-C7-F-Dm-G-Bflat-F; while the chorus is: A11-A7-Dm-C-Bflat-Gm-C-F-A11-A7-Dm-C-Bflat-Gm-C-F.

"Even if chords are simple, they should rub," says Jimmy Webb. "They should have dissonances in them.

"I've always used a lot of alternate bass lines, suspensions, widely spaced voicings, and different textures to get very warm chords," explained Webb. "Sometimes you set up strange chords by placing a chord in front of it that's going to set it off like a diamond in a gold band."

# # # #

#55
WHERE'S THE HOOK?

WHETHER YOU'RE pitching your songs to a music publisher, an A&R rep or direct to a record producer—or perhaps trying to sell your music direct to fans through iTunes or your own website—your songs must have one essential ingredient to help them sell ... a memorable HOOK that will get inside the listener's head.

A musical hook is the line in a song—usually the title line in the chorus—that really stands out and lets people know what the song is called. It's the one line (both melodically and lyrically) that people should be able to remember long after the song has finished.

Many established songwriters (especially topliners) concentrate on writing the hook before they even start working on the verse and the chorus.

They often build the rest of the song around the hook because they know it's the most important part. Some writers even keep 'hook books'—notebooks full of hook ideas and catchy musical phrases.

Unfortunately, writers who are just starting out often don't understand the importance of building an easy-to-remember, attention-grabbing hook into their songs.

They don't realize that the craft of songwriting involves telling the song's story in the verse whilst musically building tension that peaks and resolves itself in the hook in the chorus. Without this 'payoff', listeners may not feel satisfied by the song.

Failing to make sure a song has a strong, frequently repeated hook also means you're making it harder for listeners to easily understand and remember the song when they hear it for the first time.

Whatever style of music you're writing, if you have a great hook that expresses in just a few words and notes what the song is all about, then you'll have the starting point for a great song.

How do you know if you've written a great hook? Try playing it to friends and relatives and see if they can hum it afterwards. And if you can't remember the hook yourself the next day, it can't be that great!

Always keep in mind, memorable hooks are what music publishers, record labels, producers and artists are all looking for. If they don't hear a killer hook inside the first 60 seconds of your demo, they may not bother listening to the rest of the song.

In fact, the boss of one dance label reckons you have even less time than that to hook the listener. "People on average give a song seven seconds on the radio before they change the channel," he said. "So it's not enough to have one hook anymore. You've got to have a hook in the intro, a hook in the pre-chorus, a hook in the chorus, and a hook in the bridge."

# # # #

#56
PUTTING YOUR HOOK IN THE WRONG PLACE

YOUR CHANCES of having a hit will be substantially increased if you write a great hook that makes it easy for listeners to remember your song. But you still have to make sure you put the hook line in the right part of the song so that it will stand out and grab the listener's attention.

A musical hook is usually a short, catchy melodic phrase that contains the song's title. In more than half of all hit songs, the hook phrase is only about three words long. But what matters most is where you put those few words and notes in the structure of the song.

Most hit songwriters believe the hook should be the ultimate destination of the verse and pre-chorus, both lyrically and melodically. That's why, in the verse-chorus format of most of today's pop songs, it is usually placed in the first line or the last line of the chorus. It is rarely located in the middle of the chorus, or in the verse, where it is much harder for a hook line to stand out.

Melodically, the hook should cover a wide interval—perhaps a fifth or more—to give it greater impact. And it must be repeated several times throughout the song to make sure it gets inside the listener's head.

If you carefully analyze some of today's hit songs, you will spot the phrase in each song that really stands out and is familiar to you by the end of the song. That's the hook. Look at where it is located in the song. Is it in the first line of the chorus, or the last line? Is it also the title line? Is the title placed at the beginning or the end of the line? How many times is the hook repeated throughout the song?

By dissecting and analyzing hit writers' songs in this way, you will quickly learn how great hooks work. And you'll soon begin to know instinctively where to place your own hooks.

# # # #

#57
A LYRICAL HOOK THAT DOESN'T STICK

THE HOOK is meant to be a simple line that is so catchy (both musically and lyrically) that it immediately grabs the listener's attention and gets inside his or her head. But writers who are just starting out often create a hook phrase that is too long and too complicated for listeners to remember easily.

You can't just write a melody for the title line in your chorus and call it 'the hook'. If the melody and lyrics don't stick in the listener's mind, it's not a hook. And many music publishers and A&R reps will reject a song if the hook doesn't have 'stickability'.

It's hard to define what makes a hook 'catchy' and 'sticky', but it all comes down to creating a short lyrical and musical phrase that brings together connected sounds that are instantly memorable. For example, clever use of alliteration can make a hook lyric easier to remember—especially if you're looking to create a sing-along or anthemic hook.

The hook line should also have a different melodic construction from the rest of the song so that it stands out.

Listen closely to the hooks from some of today's biggest hits and you'll see how simple and short they are.

More than half of all hit songs have a hook phrase that is no more than three words and four beats long. You'll also hear how successful writers make their hook even more memorable by repeating it many times throughout the song. The more they repeat it, the more it sticks.

When you're writing a lyrical hook, remember that simplicity goes hand in hand with repetition. The song's title is the only information you need to include in the hook. The song's story should be told in the verses.

It is also important to build instant familiarity into the words used in a lyrical hook.

That's why so many song title hooks are derived from sayings and phrases that we hear every day. Something so familiar is reassuring to the listener and, subconsciously, makes the song easier to follow—increasing its 'stickability'.

# # # #

#58
RELYING ON A GOOD HOOK TO SAVE A BAD SONG

THE ABILITY to keep coming up with catchy, memorable hooks is a valuable skill that will increase your chances of songwriting success. But don't make the mistake of believing that writing an outstanding hook will automatically result in a great song.

An average song with a great hook is still an average song.

A distinctive hook line is an important part of any song because it helps to communicate what you're trying to say and makes it easier for the listener to remember what you're saying. But any weaknesses elsewhere in the song can't be fixed by adding an amazing lyrical hook, or an infectious instrumental or production hook. Music professionals will still judge your talent on the whole song.

You still need a well-structured verse that tells an interesting story and gives the song substance, plus an exciting pre-chorus that propels listeners into the chorus itself, and a contrasting bridge that gives your song an extra lift and an additional point of interest.

Many top writers start with a killer hook and then build all of the other sections around it—rather than trying to find a hook that will help make an existing song sound stronger.

If you've got a great chorus-based hook but you're struggling to find a verse that lives up to the quality of the chorus, here's a trick I've suggested to many of my songwriters over the years:

Take a chorus hook that you've written for another incomplete song and use it as the basis of the VERSE for the song you're trying to finish.

In other words, the chord progression and melody from the chorus of Song 2 becomes the verse for Song 1 (obviously you'll need to put them in the same key and add new lyrics). This simple solution could result in a very commercial song because it will have both a catchy verse and an easy-to-remember chorus!

# # # #

#59
DON'T FORGET YOUR SECONDARY HOOKS

"Great melody over great riffs is, to me, the secret of it all."
—Steven Tyler

IF YOUR ambition is to write hit singles for today's pop market, it is important to build as many different types of hooks into your songs as possible to keep listeners interested.

While a chorus-based hook is the most common and most effective device for making your song easy to remember, you can also grab the ear of the listener by including several secondary hooks, or 'sub-hooks'. They usually take the form of short instrumental phrases or riffs that are placed in the intro, between lyric lines, between verses, or after each chorus.

These infectious 'riff hooks' can be repeated several times throughout the song to reinforce the all-important lyrical and melodic hook in the chorus. Hit songs that have used this approach include Jay-Z's 'Can I Get A...', 'Beat It' by Michael Jackson, Stevie Wonder's 'Superstition', and 'Something' by The Beatles, amongst many others.

Sub-hooks can also take the form of rhythmic chord movements or a catchy extra chord change.

You can also create mini-hooks for the singer by repeating short melodic phrases within the verse melody.

Lyrics can also be used to create a sub-hook. For example, the repetition of sounds within the same line can make a lyric catchy, memorable and pleasing on the ear – and listeners will be waiting for it when the next verse comes around.

Alliteration—the repetition of a particular sound in the stressed syllables at the beginning of adjacent words or phrases (such as "Mary, marry me in the morning")—is a highly effective device that can make a lyric line stand out as a memorable hook in its own right.

Other tools that can help to catch the listener's attention include assonance (the repetition of vowel sounds to create internal rhyming within phrases—e.g. "without you I'm blue"), and consonance (the repetition of the same consonant two or more times in short succession—such as "pitter patter").

While lyrical and melodic hooks are your responsibility, don't make the mistake of leaving it to the musicians or the producer to create instrumental, rhythmic or other sound hooks. You should try out ideas for secondary hooks yourself while you're writing the song. It will save valuable time at the demo stage.

# # # #

#60
AN INTRO THAT DOESN'T ATTRACT ATTENTION

THESE DAYS, the introduction (or 'intro') is usually a short instrumental phrase or riff that opens a song. It's a kind of catchy melodic hook that is meant to have an immediate impact and is usually about four bars long.

Its purpose is to get people interested in the song—like a sign in a shop window saying: "Come inside, we've got just what you're looking for".

However, many new writers waste this golden opportunity to invite listeners to step inside their song. They create self-indulgent intros that are way too long and much too complicated to make listeners sit up and take notice.

Music publishers, A&R reps and record producers don't have the time or patience to sit through long boring intros. They may give up before your song even gets to the first verse. What they want to hear is a dynamic, memorable intro that quickly establishes the vibe, tempo and home key of the song and prepares them for the first verse.

An intro can be based on an important musical phrase from the main body of the song. Or it can be a catchy, stand-alone riff, written especially for the intro. Either way, listeners should be able to recognize it within the first couple of seconds after the song starts.

Not all songs have instrumental intros, of course. Some songs may open with the chorus, a solo vocal, or go straight into the first verse. But if you feel your song needs an intro, you must approach it as if you were writing a melodic hook for the chorus. In other words, try to create a short intro hook with 'stickability'.

# # # #

#61
AN INTRO THAT IS TOO LONG

INEXPERIENCED WRITERS often feel that the perfect way to set the stage for their first verse is to tease the listener with a long, intricate instrumental section designed to create a feeling of anticipation.

WRONG!

If you're trying to write a song with commercial potential, it's important to understand how little time you have to attract the listener's attention at the beginning of the song.

A short dynamic intro that leads quickly into the first verse is the key to pulling the listener in.

An intro that is too long will simply take up valuable time and slow down the listener's journey to the all-important first chorus. Remember, for maximum impact, you need to take the listener through the first verse and into the first chorus within 45-60 seconds.

So how long should an intro be?

An analysis of today's hit songs shows that introductions are usually either four bars or eight bars long, and, on average, last for about 10 seconds. That's only fractionally shorter than the intros of many chart hits in the 1970s. So the intro element of pop song structure has barely changed in over 40 years.

Of course, some intros are longer than 10 seconds, but few last for more than 17-20 seconds and most songs reach the first verse before the 15-second mark.

If you're a singer-songwriter, or writing for your own band, you will be able to get away with much longer intros when playing your songs live on stage. But when submitting songs to music publishers, A&R reps or record producers, it is best to limit the intros on your demo to 10 seconds or less—so that those who are judging your talent can get to the substance of each song as quickly as possible.

# # # #

#62
NOT ADMIRING THE VIEW FROM THE BRIDGE

"If after two weeks you still can't write your middle-eight, the best course of action is to see a psychiatrist"
—Ray Davies

NOT INCLUDING a bridge (or 'middle-eight') is another common mistake made by new songwriters.

The bridge can be an effective device for adding extra contrast to a song and giving listeners a temporary release from the heavily repeated phrases in the verse, chorus and hook.

The bridge can provide a whole different perspective—'the view from the bridge'—by allowing you to introduce chord progressions, melodic phrases and lyrics that aren't heard anywhere else in the song.

The bridge section is usually limited to four or eight bars of music and two or four lines of lyrics. It is commonly used only once—replacing what listeners might expect to be a third verse—before leading the listener into the repeated choruses at the end of the song.

The bridge itself can be repeated (especially in the verse-refrain format), but it rarely appears more than twice.

The standard formats for songs that use a bridge are:

1. Verse, Chorus, Verse, Chorus, BRIDGE, Chorus, Chorus.

2. Verse, Pre-Chorus, Chorus, Verse, Pre-Chorus, Chorus, BRIDGE, Chorus, Chorus.

3. Verse, Refrain, Verse, Refrain, BRIDGE, Verse, Refrain, Refrain.

Some hit songwriters make their bridge section melodically different by changing the length of the notes and making them either higher or lower in the scale than those in the chorus or verse. Other writers even include a slight key change in the bridge before leading listeners back to the chorus repeats.

You can surprise the listener by changing the lyrical cadence and even the rhyme pattern in the bridge.

This section can also be used to set things up lyrically for the end of the song, perhaps by adding a new dimension to your storyline (such as a twist or a new revelation in the lyrics).

However, unlike the chorus, the bridge should only be used to provide new information and not just re-state something that has already been said.

For example, the bridge should not include the song's title. Keep the title line in the hook in the chorus.

And if you find your song is too short, a bridge is a great way to stretch it by an extra 20-30 seconds—whilst strengthening the song melodically and lyrically at the same time.

Of course, not all songs have a bridge section. There are many hit songs that are bridge-less. But if you're heavily repeating certain musical phrases and lyrics to make your song catchy and easier to remember, you can prevent it from becoming too repetitive by shaking things up with a bridge.

# # # #

#63
NOT BUILDING ON THE VERSE AND CHORUS WITH YOUR BRIDGE

"On a bridge, if you can surprise the listener it's going to stay with him longer and it won't just be a point in the song when the listener's ear is vamping waiting to get back to the song's main melody"
—Roger Nichols

SOME WRITERS make the mistake of treating the bridge as a throwaway section that is simply there to give listeners a brief release from the verses and the chorus. In fact, a good bridge has a number of very important functions.

An effective bridge can add extra impact and sustain the listener's interest by building on the energy and drama created in the verse and chorus.

The bridge can surprise the listener by taking the song in a completely different direction both melodically and lyrically. In effect, it's a mini-song within the main song. It should use a four or eight bar melody and chord progression that is not heard anywhere else in the song, and it must add new information to the song's storyline (perhaps an unexpected twist).

Many successful writers give their songs a lift, and achieve an element of surprise, by starting their bridge section on a minor chord when writing in a major key (for example, starting the bridge on A minor if the song is in the key of C).

If it is constructed correctly, the bridge melody should then lead the listener back to the all-important chorus and hook. When you analyze current hit songs that have a bridge, you'll find that, in many cases, the bridge ends on the dominant chord (e.g. G in the key of C) which paves the way for an emotional return to the 'home' chord (C) at the start of the chorus repeats.

# # # #

#64
BUILDING YOUR BRIDGE IN THE WRONG PLACE

THE ROLE of the bridge section is to surprise listeners by suddenly (and briefly) taking the song in a completely different direction, both melodically and lyrically. As in any ambush, therefore, the bridge has to be positioned strategically at the point where it will have the greatest impact.

When using a song structure that includes verses and repeated choruses, the optimum location for the bridge is about two-thirds of the way into the song—usually between the second and third choruses.

This is the point at which listeners may start to get bored by the repetition of the verses and chorus.

For example:
1. Verse, Chorus, Verse, Chorus, BRIDGE, Chorus, Chorus.
2. Verse, Pre-Chorus, Chorus, Verse, Pre-Chorus, Chorus, BRIDGE, Chorus, Chorus.

As you can see, the chorus after the bridge is usually the first of the chorus repeats at the end of the song.

If your song doesn't include a separate chorus, the bridge should ideally be placed between the second and third verses (for example: Verse, Verse, BRIDGE, Verse).

With the verse-only structure, if you find your song is too short, you can stretch it by 20-30 seconds by repeating the bridge like a mini-chorus (e.g. Verse, Verse, BRIDGE, Verse, BRIDGE, Verse).

# # # #

#65
NOT USING A PRE-CHORUS TO BUILD TENSION

SOME WRITERS make the mistake of using a pre-chorus purely as a way of linking the last line of the verse and the first line of the chorus. A pre-chorus is optional, of course, but if you're going to use this device, you have to make sure it's much more than just a short melodic bridge between the verse and the main chorus.

Although a pre-chorus is usually a two or four-line section that is rarely more than four bars long, it should be used to create a powerful melodic tension at the end of the verse that is only resolved when the chorus kicks in.

Like the bridge section later in the song, the pre-chorus melody should be distinctive and different from the preceding lines of the verse.

It is meant to provide a musical ladder that enables the lower notes of the verse melody to climb up to the higher and more powerful pitches used in the all-important chorus and hook.

The pre-chorus melody should be the same every time, although the lyrics may change as the story builds.

Hit songwriters use this technique to add a burst of extra energy. It can increase excitement and tension, and create a feeling of anticipation before propelling the listener into the chorus.

That's why the pre-chorus is also referred to as a 'build', 'lift', 'climb', 'set up', 'channel' or 'pre-hook'. Each of these terms accurately describes its important role as a means of building momentum and drawing the listener's attention to the start of the chorus.

If you analyze the pre-chorus section of some of today's biggest hits, you'll find it often sounds like you've already reached the chorus—then the real chorus suddenly bursts in and hits you between the eyes. The tension and subsequent sense of release that this creates helps to make the hook even more impactful.

# # # #

#66
FAILING TO MAKE YOUR CHORUS STAND OUT

*"The chorus to me is the gist of the song; that's where the idea is delivered …
If I don't get the chorus right, it's no use in me writing the song"*
—Toby Keith

THE CHORUS is the section that is meant to really sell a song.

But one of the most common traps that new songwriters fall into is creating a chorus that sounds too much like the verse and therefore isn't distinctive enough to stand out from the rest of the song.

If your chorus doesn't contain the most memorable melody and lyrics in the whole song, it is unlikely to get stuck in the listener's head and won't sustain his or her interest.

A chorus that is based on the same set of four or five notes as the verse may lack a unique shape. This can result in a song that resembles a flat, boring landscape with no dramatic peaks that stand out and fill the listener with awe.

So how do you create a standout chorus that lifts the energy level and keeps the song memorable?

Firstly, there has to be a significant difference between the verse melody and the chorus melody. One of the most effective ways of achieving this is to build a 'lift' into the chorus melody by placing the chorus higher in the scale than the verse. Many hit songwriters even change to a higher key at the chorus to make it stand out and give the hook extra potency.

Using the same chord progression in the verse and chorus can also make both sections sound too similar, even if you write the verse in a lower melodic range. So surprise the listener.

—Use a different chord sequence that involves more (or fewer) chord changes than in the verse.

—Make the first chord of your chorus different from the first chord of the verse.

—Make the number of lines in the chorus different from the number of lines in the verse.

—Make sure the last chord of the chorus is different from the first chord of the verse.

— Make the rhyming pattern of the chorus lyrics and the cadence of the syllables different from the verse.

— Make the information conveyed in the chorus simple enough for people to remember the words easily.

The chorus should also contain a big 'pay-off' line in order to give the listener a sense of satisfaction and completion. The pay-off is usually the hook or title line and can come at the beginning or the end of the chorus. It should pack a big punch to add extra emotional impact.

You can also make the chorus stand out—and really drive it home—by repeating it several times throughout the song. If you analyze some of today's hit songs, you'll find that the chorus is often repeated at least four times ... and even more frequently in many dance-oriented pop songs.

#67
IMBALANCE BETWEEN VERSE AND CHORUS LYRICS

WHEN WRITING in the verse-chorus format, some new writers weaken the overall structure of their songs by not achieving the right balance between their verse lyrics and chorus lyrics.

The lyrics in your verses should be mostly descriptive (describing people, places and events), while the chorus lyrics should be mainly emotional (delivering a strong emotional reaction to what has just been described in the verse).

Each verse should move the song's storyline forward like a new chapter in a book, introducing fresh information and images that will captivate the listener.

The chorus, meanwhile, is meant to really drive home the whole point of your song—for example, by frequently repeating the title line like a catchphrase. It's the section where your message should become clear and memorable.

You can also help to emphasize the chorus by making the rhyming pattern of the lyrics—and even the cadence of the syllables—substantially different from those in the verse. The verse may be filled with abundant and meaningful words (with more notes per beat), but the chorus lyrics should be lighter and less crowded.

To achieve the greatest impact, the chorus needs a simpler meter, fewer syllables, and longer notes to help more emotional lyrics register with listeners.

All of this means the information conveyed in the chorus can be much more general and philosophical, making it easier for people to remember the words.

Moving back and forth between these two different types of lyrics can help to create an extra level of contrast between the verse and chorus in addition to the differences that you are already creating melodically.

THINKING POEMS AND SONG LYRICS ARE THE SAME

"Lyrics have elements that could be shared with poetry. But they're not poems ... They're meant to be sung. They come out of the rhythm of the music, as opposed to creating your own rhythm of the words"
—Paul Simon

MANY NEW songwriters don't realize that poetry and lyrics are not the same thing. However great you or your collaborators may be at creating beautiful poetry, writing effective lyrics for hit songs is a completely different art and craft.

Of course, good poetry and great lyrics do share the same ability to use well-chosen words to reach people on an emotional level. And they can both create powerful imagery through the potent use of devices such as metaphor, simile and personification.

But the skilful use of language, rhyme and descriptive imagery in a poem does not necessarily make it a good song lyric. Sometimes it can just end up sounding pretentious and clichéd.

Lyricists have to work their magic under much tighter constraints than poets. A poet can pour out his or her feelings on page after page of dense and structurally complex text; the lyricist has to be more concise and work within the confines of a clearly defined song structure and rhythm.

"Lyrics are an unforgivingly compact form", the lyricist Stephen Sondheim wrote in his book *Finishing the Hat.*

It is also important to remember that a poem is primarily visual. It is created to stand alone and connect with people by being read on the page. A lyric is aural and is designed to be sung and heard in conjunction with music.

As Bob Dylan once told *American Songwriter* magazine: "You don't write a song to sit there on a page. You write it to sing it."

When people are listening to a song, the music moves quickly so they can't dwell on a particular word or line. Unlike a poem—which is usually read at a much slower pace—they can't go back and re-read it.

While some song lyrics may be deliberately obscure and ambiguous and still succeed (such as the early works of Bob Dylan), the majority of hit songs today contain lyrical images and descriptive phrases that are easily understood and can therefore connect with the listener's ears immediately.

Lyrical language is simpler, more down to earth and gets to the point quickly. In a 3½ to 4 minute pop song, every word counts. So it's vital to use as few words as possible yet still express yourself clearly, set the scene, and evoke a feeling in the listener.

Poems can feature rhymed or unrhymed verse, but most lyrics have lines that rhyme because it makes it easier for listeners to follow the song. As mentioned previously in this book, rhyme helps to meet the listener's subconscious desire for symmetry. Rhyming patterns create a sense of predictability that is reassuring for the listener.

A poet can focus on the creative use of free-flowing language, but a good lyricist must learn to use the key structural devices of the craft of songwriting (including lyrical repetition). Lyricists must also understand how verses, pre-choruses, choruses and bridges work together to hold the listener's interest.

In addition, if you aspire to be the wordsmith in a songwriting team, you have to make sure you use word sounds and phrases that are not difficult or awkward to sing. If you're writing the lyrics first—rather than coming up with words to fit an existing melody—get into the habit of reading the lyrics out loud rhythmically as if you were singing them. If they flow well, your collaborative music composer should be able to set them to music successfully.

# # # #

#69
THINKING LYRICS DON'T MATTER AS LONG AS THE MUSIC IS GOOD

WHILE IT'S true that the melody and the title are regarded as the most important parts of a song, don't make the mistake of believing that the quality of the lyrics doesn't really matter if your song has a strong melody, a catchy hook and great beats.

Don't ever settle for lyrics that you know are second-best. A song with a dynamic melody and trite lyrics is still unlikely to be successful.

Of course, songs with weak lyrics occasionally do well in the charts, but their success is usually down to an outstanding production or because the artist concerned is already a big star with a loyal fan base.

If you're an aspiring new writer submitting a demo to a music publisher, A&R rep or a record producer, you'll need more than just an excellent melody to stimulate their interest.

You have to be able to offer them a complete work that combines a highly commercial melody with well-chosen words and descriptive phrases that make sense and actually say something.

Music industry professionals expect to hear inventive lyrics that avoid clichés and convey an interesting story or message in an easily understandable way.

They want words that support the title and the hook, and evoke an emotional response within the listener.

As a music publisher, there is nothing more frustrating than taking the time to listen to a demo by a new writer only to find that a promising melody is weakened by lyrics that seem to have been thrown together with little thought. The irritation that this causes often results in even the most generous music pros hitting the 'stop' button after about 30 seconds!

If you're very lucky, they might see that you potentially have half a hit song and may ask you re-write the lyrics and re-submit the revised song. At worst, they may assume that every song they receive from you in future will have equally poor lyrics … and they won't even bother listening.

# # # #

#70
YOUR LYRICS DON'T SUPPORT THE SONG FORM

WRITING LYRICS that don't support the form of a song in the verse-chorus format is one of the most common songwriting errors. New writers often don't realize that the verse and the chorus have different responsibilities and that the lyrics in each section need to reflect this.

If you listen closely to the lyrics of today's most successful songs, you will find that the verses mostly use descriptive words (telling a story, describing people and situations, or showing the singer's state of mind), while the chorus lyrics mainly express emotions. They provide an emotional response to what has just been described in the verse.

Look on the verse-chorus song structure as a roadmap, with the verse as a scenic highway and the chorus as the 'big city-bright lights' destination.

Your main focus in the verse, therefore, should be to use descriptive words in a linear and conversational way to set the scene and then move the song's storyline forward. Balance your lyrics by saving strong emotions for the chorus.

As you drive toward the chorus, you can introduce fresh information and images in each line to attract and hold the listener's interest. First verses usually provide the broad strokes necessary to set the stage for the rest of the song, while the subsequent verses can be more specific.

The chorus, meanwhile, is the section where the whole point of your song should become clear and memorable. You should be able to use simpler and more emotional words because the verse has already built a firm foundation and filled in all the details—allowing the chorus to focus on hammering home the title and the all-important hook.

# # # #

#71
YOUR LYRIC LINES AREN'T BALANCED

Some writers construct songs based on short lines of lyrics, while others have longer lines with more beats. There is no fixed rule, although it's usually much easier to write a good melody for a lyric that has shorter lines.

But what you should never do is make the mistake of using a different line length in the corresponding line in each verse or chorus!

To achieve the musical symmetry that is so important to listeners' ears, it is essential to make sure that your lyrics are balanced and don't have uneven line lengths or syllable counts. It's the same as ensuring that all your verses have exactly the same number of bars and your pre-chorus and chorus are the same length every time.

When you analyze the structure of your favorite writers' songs, you will find they usually have the same number of syllables between corresponding lines.

For example, if the first line of their first verse has eight syllables, then the first line of their second verse will also have eight syllables.

Similarly, if a verse or a chorus consists of four lines, then every line should have the same number of syllables. If the amount differs, it may create a distracting imbalance for the listener.

#72
TOO MANY WORDS IN YOUR LYRICS

SQUEEZING TOO many words into a lyric is one of the most common mistakes made by inexperienced songwriters—especially writers or lyricists who aren't singers themselves.

They don't realize the importance of leaving pauses between the words so that the poor singer can grab a breath!

If your lyric lines are too crowded, singers will be so busy trying to fit all the words in that they won't have space to emphasize the key words—and won't be able to interpret the song in their own distinctive way.

Putting too many words into your song also makes it harder for listeners to take in the lyrics and understand what the song is about. It's like someone talking so fast you can't grasp what they're saying. People have to be able to make out every word that you've worked so hard to craft—otherwise, what's the point?

As Paul Simon told *American Songwriter* magazine: "When you're reading poetry, you read it at a much slower pace. So the lines can be much more dense, and have words which are not usually in a speaking vocabulary, and which carry multiple meanings. But in a song, it's clocking along, and if you missed it, it's gone. And if you miss enough of it, well, the song is gone …".

To make it easier for listeners to remember your lyrics, it's important to keep them simple and conversational.

The great lyricist Hal David, for example, was a master at conveying what he wanted to say in the most concise way possible, despite the complexity of some of Burt Bacharach's melodies.

It's all part of the craft of successful songwriting.

Even if you're not a great vocalist, try singing the song yourself at the tempo it's supposed to be played at. Or read the lyrics out loud rhythmically, keeping time as if you were singing them. If you can't fit all the words in comfortably—with the key words accentuated—it's likely that an experienced singer won't be able to do it either.

This will hamper your chances of getting other artists to record the song. And if you're writing for your own band, even your own superb vocalist may find it hard to impress your fans!

If your lyrics are a maze of words, it will be hard for any performance of them to be amazing.

# # # #

#73
NOT PAINTING A PICTURE

BE CAREFUL not to bore listeners by simply pouring out fact after fact in your lyrics as you tell the song's story. You have to choose words that paint a picture in their imagination so that you can reach them on an emotional level and make them feel what you're feeling (or what the singer is feeling).

This aspect of the craft of successful songwriting is a major challenge because you have to skillfully use powerful devices such as metaphor, simile, personification and rhyme within the constraints of a clearly defined song structure and rhythm. And you only have three minutes or so in which to get some vivid colors onto your lyrical canvas to captivate the listener.

That's why many top writers' lyrical language is simpler and more down to earth—with short lyrical images and colorful descriptive phrases that are easily understood and can therefore immediately connect with the listener.

Remember, as well as painting a picture for the listener you still need to get them to the all-important hook in the chorus within 45-60 seconds!

#74
A CLICHÉ TOO FAR

"I try to avoid certain images that I feel have been done to death, such as any reference to angels or hearts ... and use of the word baby"
—Aimee Mann

WHEN MUSIC publishers, A&R executives and producers listen to a demo of a new song, one of the most common reasons why they end up hitting the 'stop' button is because they find the song's lyrics are too full of clichés.

Remember, by the time these music industry pros get to hear your demo they've probably already listened to thousands of songs during their careers. So they literally have heard it all before. They've had to endure all the old worn-out lines—all the overly familiar descriptions, tired phrases and metaphors, and predictable rhymes (such as "kiss you...miss you") ... and then some.

Many of these lines were originally created by great lyricists, of course, but they've been reused and misused so many times over the years that they have now become boring clichés. If someone is going to sign your song, or cut it with their artist, they want to hear lyrics that are fresh and inventive—with some original rhymes or a new twist on an old theme.

"Most lyricists rely too much on the standard rock clichés," Aimee Mann once remarked. "Good writers turn the clichés around."

One of the finest examples of this is Diane Warren's song 'Un-Break My Heart' which was a huge hit for Toni Braxton in 1996. The phrase "break my heart" must have been used thousands of times since the dawn of the music industry. But Diane Warren turned the cliché on its head and created something brand new that really made the song stand out.

"The title popped into my head," she explained, "and I thought, 'I don't think I've heard that before, that's kind of interesting'."

The takeaway from this is: if there's a line you plan to use and you've already heard it in another song, push yourself to find a new way of saying it so that it will have greater impact and create a much stronger image in the listener's head. And don't be ashamed to turn to a dictionary or a thesaurus for help.

When the great Steven Sondheim was once asked how he came up with his rhymes, he admitted: "I use a rhyming dictionary". Other top writers also keep a dictionary of synonyms handy.

Jimmy Webb, in his book *Tunesmith: Inside the Art of Songwriting*, observed: "There is one thing that these gentlemen and ladies [great lyricists] have in common, whatever their style. Virtually all of them keep a rhyming dictionary and a thesaurus close by. No shame here. In fact it is not a very lucid act to attempt the writing of verse in any form without these unless one happens to be a Mensa."

# # # #

#75
YOUR FIRST LINE COULD BE YOUR LAST

"I was washing dishes at the Greyhound bus station at the time and I said, 'A-wop-bom-a-loo-mop-a-lomp-bam-boom, take 'em out!'"
—Little Richard

ALTHOUGH A song's title is its strongest selling point and the best way to attract people's attention, many inexperienced writers don't realize that the lyrical content of their song's opening line can play an equally important role in stimulating the listener's interest and creating a lasting impact.

When busy publishers, A&R executives or producers play your demo and hear your opening line for the first time, they're already deciding whether or not to hit the 'stop' button. So you've got maybe 10 seconds in which to convince them to keep listening.

While the title should tell people what your song is all about in just one word or a single phrase, the opening line of the first verse should be just as memorable and interesting (both musically and lyrically). Ideally, it should create a visual image that stimulates the listener's imagination and paves the way for the story that follows.

How many classic songs have stuck in your mind over the years because you remember the first line of the lyrics as well as the title line?

It could be a catchy opening line like "Well, she was just seventeen – you know what I mean" (from 'I Saw Her Standing There' by The Beatles) ... or an intriguing metaphor or personification like Paul Simon's "Hello, Darkness, my old friend" (from Simon and Garfunkel's 'The Sound of Silence') ... or sensory imagery such as "On a dark desert highway, cool wind in my hair" (from The Eagles' 'Hotel California').

A play on similar word sounds can also be effective, such as Little Richard's classic "A-wop-bom-a-loo-mop-a-lomp-bam-boom" from 'Tutti Frutti' (described by *Rolling Stone* magazine as "the most inspired rock lyric ever recorded").

Engaging first lines such as these instantly draw listeners into a song and hook their interest.

Listen again to a few songs by your favorite writers and make a note of the opening line in each case. Analyze the structure of the line and the writer's choice of words. See how it works like a mini hook and sets the stage for the rest of the song. Then apply what you learn to the first couple of lines of your own songs.

# # # #

NOT LETTING YOUR SONG MOVE FORWARD

"I find second verses really hard. Third verses are sometimes like pulling teeth, but by then you're in the home stretch, you just hit the wall and go through"
—Janis Ian

BE CAREFUL not to fall into the common trap of writing a great first line and then, without realizing it, simply restating that line in different ways throughout the rest of the song.

Every word in every subsequent line should be carefully chosen to move the song forward, rather than merely creating nice word pictures that don't actually lead anywhere.

Approach each new verse as if you were a screenwriter creating a sequence of movie scenes. Build on your central storyline by focusing on a specific scenario in each verse so that it ties in with the previous 'scene' and the one that follows. Adding new and relevant information in each line of every verse in this way is essential to progressing the story.

In other words, the second verse and third verse (if there is one) should not just say the same thing that you said in the first verse. They must tell the listener what happened next, or provide more information about the central characters in the song, or expand on your description of the singer's state of mind.

The best way to make sure the various sections fit together and give your lyrics a linear flow is to produce a 'map' of the song.

Create a simple flowchart on a piece of paper by drawing a separate box for each different part of the song, with an arrow leading to the next section (e.g. Verse 1—Chorus—Verse 2—Chorus—Verse 3—Chorus—Bridge—Chorus).

In each box, insert a phrase that summarizes the main point that you want to convey lyrically in that section. The lyrics should be the same in every chorus; so only the verses and the bridge will change as the story moves forward.

If you find you're struggling to come up with something new to say in the second and third verses, don't worry. You're not alone. Even top songwriters often find the lyrics for the second verse are the hardest to write. They call it "second verse hell".

However, experienced writers have a simple way of overcoming this block.

If they've completed the lyrics for their first verse and chorus—and there seems to be nowhere else to go because everything they wanted to say has already been said—they simply make the first verse their second verse. This means they have to come up with another first verse!

# # # #

#77
WRITING LYRICS PEOPLE CAN'T RELATE TO

"Rock isn't art, it's the way ordinary people talk"
—Billy Idol

A COMMON mistake among many new writers is their use of over-elaborate imagery and 'poetic' lyrics in an attempt to show how clever and creative they can be. Far from being impressed, though, music publishers and A&R reps are more likely to see unnecessarily flowery language as a sign of inexperience.

Trying too hard to be 'different' and artistic can often result in lyrics that simply sound pretentious and self-indulgent. If your lyrics don't come across as genuine, listeners may find it hard to connect with your song.

To be successful, a song must be able to reach out and touch listeners and make them feel something.

This means your song needs to be about something that everyone is familiar with—and your lyrics should be honest, believable and heartfelt so that people can easily relate to them.

One way to achieve this is to write as if you're having a one-on-one conversation with the listener. It's okay to separate contractions, or leave out unimportant words such as 'that', if it makes the line sound like it could be spoken naturally.

"I try to write conversationally," The Eagles' Don Henley once said. "I try to write like people speak and put the emphasis on the right syllable."

This musical 'conversation' requires lyrics that, ideally, should be simple, straightforward and contemporary. As Don Henley showed in many of his songs, you can still create powerful imagery through devices such as metaphor, simile and personification, but there should be no forced rhymes and no tangled and complex phrases or sentences that don't make sense to the listener.

As Emeli Sandé sees it: "You have to be honest and true about what you're writing, and then that way it resonates with people."

# # # #

#78
NOT MAINTAINING A CONSISTENT VIEWPOINT

WITHOUT REALIZING it, some developing songwriters fail to maintain the same viewpoint throughout their lyrics because they are not consistent in their use of pronouns such as I, Me, We, Us, He, She, Them, They and You.

Switching pronouns in mid-song can make your lyrics unclear. And if the viewpoint of your song keeps changing in this way, there is a danger that listeners will end up getting confused—and may simply switch off.

When you start working on a new song, it is important to decide upfront which viewpoint the singer is meant to take when performing the song. Will the singer being singing about himself or herself … or singing about someone else … or singing to someone else? The viewpoint you choose will determine which personal pronouns, subject pronouns, object pronouns, etc. should be used throughout the song.

The most common mistake is when a writer takes a third person perspective in the first verse (i.e. singing about someone – He, She, Them, They – but not directly to them) and then, in the second verse, shifts either to a first person narrative (I, We, He, She, They, Us), or to a second person viewpoint (i.e. singing directly to a specific person).

If you take a third person perspective in the first verse ('He did this' or 'She did that'), then all subsequent verses should also have a third person viewpoint.

These days, most songs tend to be in the first person (I, Me, We, Us), with the singer talking to someone else (You) in a conversational style. A song becomes much more personal when 'You' and 'I' are used.

Whichever viewpoint you use, however, it is essential to keep your pronouns consistent. Make sure each character in the song is represented by the same pronoun each time, both in the verses and the chorus. Listeners may get confused if, in the middle of the song, someone who was previously addressed as 'She' suddenly becomes 'You', or if 'He' becomes 'Me'.

One exception, though, is the bridge. Some experienced songwriters often deliberately change the viewpoint in the bridge as a means of adding something fresh to the song. But be careful not to cause any confusion if you do shift the lyrical perspective in this way.

Remember, simplicity and clarity are essential. Stick to a single viewpoint throughout the song, and always make it clear who is doing the talking or thinking.

# # # #

#79
GETTING TENSE ABOUT TENSE

BE CAREFUL not to fall into the trap of confusing listeners by not being consistent in your use of tense throughout a song.

Remember, when people hear your song, they only know what you tell them in the lyrics—so it's vital to make sure the timeframe for a song is always clear and easy to follow.

This means all lyric lines should be in the same tense instead of time-traveling between past, present and future from line to line.

The consistent use of tense is important because it locates your song's story in a specific time and helps listeners understand when the situation or action described in the song takes place.

If the tense keeps changing, there is a danger that listeners will end up bewildered, and may simply lose interest in the song.

Getting the tense right can sometimes be a tricky business, though. Most people only think in terms of past, present or future. But, grammatically, lyricists are potentially faced with a multitude of different tenses.

For example, the **Simple Present Tense** is used to describe events, actions or situations that have started but haven't yet finished, although the lyric doesn't explain when they started or whether they're still active (e.g. "I go to pieces over you…").

The **Present Progressive Tense** is about something that is happening right now (e.g. "I'm going to pieces over you…").

The **Present Perfect Tense** draws attention to the present consequences of a past event that has now finished, as opposed to its actual occurrence (e.g. "I've gone to pieces over you…").

The **Present Perfect Progressive Tense** is used for an ongoing action in the past which continues right up to the present (or has recently finished), although the lyric doesn't explain when it started (e.g. "I've been going to pieces over you…").

The **Simple Past Tense** recounts events or actions that happened at some point in the past and are now completed (e.g. "I went to pieces over you…").

The **Past Progressive Tense** is used to describe events that were happening at a point in the past but are being talked about at this moment, and may still be happening currently (e.g. "I was going to pieces over you…").

The **Past Perfect Tense** portrays situations that had already been completed at the specific point in time that you're writing about (e.g. "I had gone to pieces over you…").

The **Past Perfect Progressive Tense** is similar to the Present Perfect Progressive, except the point in time referred to in the lyric is in the past (e.g. "I had been going to pieces over you…").

And there are many more different tenses with definitions that will make your brain ache!!

The key, though, is to decide upfront which tense you intend to use in a new song and then stick to it. As you write more songs and gain more experience, you'll start to develop an instinct for choosing the most appropriate tense for each song.

The past tense is usually ideal for story songs that have a clear flow of time. The present tense is often best for love songs or songs with a strong emotional message. According to one study, more than 80% of up-tempo hits are set in the present.

While the most effective lyrics tend to stay in one tense, it doesn't mean the event flow within your song has to be linear. For example, you can use devices such as flashbacks as long as you include a transitioning word or phrase such as "I remember when…" or "Last night…". This 'linking' phrase shows the connection between past and present and explains the change of tense to the listener.

It is quite common for hit songwriters to show how past events have impacted on a current situation by putting the first two verses in the past tense and switching to the present in the chorus and final verse (e.g. "I was going to pieces over you" (in the verse) and "But I'm over you now and my life is full of sunshine" (in the chorus).

There is often scope for changing tense in the bridge to provide a 'release' from the rest of the song.

In general, though, it is best to avoid changing tense unless it is essential to your story. The tense that you choose for your lyrics can significantly affect the way your song connects with listeners.

When you've finished writing your song, always check that the timeframe or flow of time is consistent throughout. Make sure you haven't unknowingly changed tense in places where you didn't intend to.

# # # #

#80
YOUR RHYMES ARE TOO PREDICTABLE

"The ears expect certain rhymes, so you want to fool them because one of the things you want to do in a song is surprise an audience"
—Stephen Sondheim

AS A publisher I have often listened to demos by aspiring songwriters and, despite always hoping to discover a fresh new talent, ended up feeling disappointed because I found that I could predict what the rhyme was going to be on almost every line.

Inexperienced writers often weaken potentially good songs by going for the easiest rhyme, or by using the same rhyme sound too many times in a row. This simply makes the lyrics sound boring, monotonous and colorless.

It's not enough to simply go through the alphabet looking for words that rhyme, irrespective of whether or not the chosen word helps to underpin the meaning of your song and drive the story forward. This lazy approach usually results in clichéd rhymes that we've all heard many times before.

These days, you have to be more creatively adventurous.

Historically, many pop songs in the rock era have featured 'perfect' rhymes where a one-syllable word is rhymed with another one-syllable word (such as 'kiss' and 'miss'), or where two words have the same spelling in the last syllable (such as 'love and 'above'). But hit songwriting is more sophisticated these days, and publishers and A&R reps have much higher expectations of lyricists.

In fact, many established songwriters now try to steer clear of perfect rhymes because, they say, rhymes that are too exact can limit the expression of true emotion. Using 'false' rhymes which create word pictures, or convey what you want to say more accurately, can often be much more effective than pure rhymes.

For example, today's hit writers are more likely to rhyme words that don't have the same combination of letters but sound similar (such as 'clown' and 'around', or 'made' and 'late'). This is because sound-alike words can often engage listeners more than words with the same spelling.

As Stephen Sondheim once explained: "One of the uses of rhyme is not only to focus the attention on the word, but to strengthen what you're saying. So, you don't make the least important word in the line the rhyme word."

You can also surprise the listener by having the rhyme fall on the second or third syllable of a multi-syllable word instead of at the end (i.e. put the rhyme on the syllable that is stressed most strongly in normal speech, such as 'unachievable' and 'believable').

You can also rhyme a multi-syllable word with a word that only has one syllable (such as 'sublime' and 'time'). This device can make a lyric much more interesting.

It's also okay to use a rhyming dictionary. Most top songwriters admit that they always keep a rhyming dictionary and a thesaurus handy. So don't feel it will make you any less creative. It will actually make you more adventurous and give you many more options—including multi-syllable rhyme words that you might not otherwise have thought of.

Even when you're using a rhyming dictionary, don't always go for the most obvious rhyme word.

By digging deeper, and cross-referencing with a book of synonyms, you can often discover rhymes that inspire new themes or fresh ideas that can take your lyrics in a more exciting (and less predictable) direction.

# # # #

#81
NOT VARYING YOUR RHYME PATTERNS

DON'T MAKE the mistake of using exactly the same rhyming pattern throughout your song.

It is best to vary the rhyme scheme in the verse, chorus and bridge, so that each section is different and has its own personality.

One of the most common traps that new songwriters fall into is creating a lyrical structure in the chorus that sounds too much like the verse.

Changing the rhythm of the lyric—and the pattern or placement of the rhymes—can help to underpin a strong shift in the chorus melody and give your chorus a unique shape that really makes it stand out.

As you build the song's energy in the journey from the verse to the chorus, a change in the rhyme scheme—combined with a change in the melody—can help to prepare listeners for the all-important hook in the chorus.

For example, your rhyme pattern in a four-line verse may involve making the first line rhyme with the third line, while the second and fourth lines also rhyme (this is known as an ABAB rhyme scheme and is the most common).

You can then make the chorus sound different from the verse by switching to an ABCB scheme (where only the second and fourth lines rhyme) or an AABB scheme (where the first and second lines rhyme, as do the third and fourth lines).

You can also establish a clear difference by varying the primary vowel sounds in each rhyme in the chorus—so that some rhyme lines end with long vowels and others have shorter vowel sounds.

One way of building the lyrical rhythm in the verse is to use internal rhymes. This involves repeating vowels and consonants (and combinations of both) within each individual line. For example: "I'm lost in an ocean of restless emotion that only the lonely can feel".

But don't forget, the rhyming pattern that you choose for the verse should be the same in every verse, while the rhyme scheme for the chorus and the bridge should remain the same whenever the chorus and bridge are repeated.

# # # #

#82
YOUR LYRICS WON'T MOTIVATE A SINGER

IF YOUR aim is to have your songs recorded by established artists, don't make the mistake of submitting a song that you know has weak lyrics—even if the song has an irresistible melody and a hook that is infectious and memorable.

Artists and their producers are naturally attracted to catchy songs that stand out as potential hit singles. But the subject matter is equally important.

What really motivates a singer to want to record a song—and perform it live—is an outstanding lyric that moves him or her in some way. It also has to fit with the artist's on-stage image (whether that image is 'sexy', 'cool', 'romantic' or 'rebellious').

Remember, there aren't many successful artists who don't write their own material these days. As a result, they are constantly being bombarded with demos from songwriters. Your offering will have to compete with the latest songs by some of today's best professional writers. So the bar is set extremely high.

As a song provider, your primary role will be to create distinctive songs that will help to build or sustain an artist's career. You also have to enhance the artist's appeal by coming up with fresh-sounding song themes and lyrics that will keep fans buying their records.

That's why you need imaginative lyrics that avoid clichés, but are still written in conversational contemporary language. You need an interesting storyline about situations, struggles and hardships that the artist can relate to, and which he or she can use to evoke an emotional response within their fans.

So you should never pitch a song that is just 'okay' lyrically. A song with a dynamic melody and trite lyrics is unlikely to be picked up.

If you're a solo writer, and you feel you've written a hit tune but just can't come up with a lyric that does the melody justice, maybe it's time to consider partnering with a skilled lyricist?

# # # #

#83
TOO MANY TONGUE-TWISTERS

ALLITERATION—the repetition of a particular sound in the stressed syllables at the beginning of adjacent words or phrases (such as "Mary, marry me in the morning")—is a highly effective device that can make a lyric line stand out as a memorable hook in its own right.

Other tools which can help to catch the listener's attention include: **assonance**—the repetition of vowel sounds to create internal rhyming within phrases (e.g. "without you I'm blue")—and **consonance**, the repetition of the same consonant two or more times in short succession (such as "pitter patter").

These devices can add interest to your lyrics when used sparingly. But new writers sometimes make the mistake of over-doing such clever wordplay—resulting in lyrics that may be hard to sing because they contain too many 'tongue-twisters'.

If you intend to sprinkle some clever alliteration, assonance and consonance into your songs, always consider your choice of words from the singer's perspective. There are several key points to remember if you want artists to be able to sing your songs comfortably:

—Single syllable words make a song much easier to sing.

—Accented syllables should fall on the accented notes of the melody.

—Vowels are far easier to sing and hold than consonants.

—Too many sibilants (e.g. 's', 'z', 'sh', 'ch') can cause problems, especially at the end of a word.

—Some word sounds are harder to sing at the upper or lower end of a singer's vocal range.

—Words should ideally end with sounds that open the singer's mouth, not close it.

Of course, some songs are intended to twist singers' tongues—such as the 1908 classic 'She Sells Sea-shells on the Sea-shore' (words by British songwriter Terry Sullivan and music by Harry Gifford), or Sylvia Fine's 'Tongue Twisters' recorded by Danny Kaye in 1951. More recently, Ed Sheeran had a go with his song 'You Need Me, I Don't Need You'.

# # # #

PART 4:

RE-WRITING

#84
NOT USING ENOUGH POLISH

"Great songs aren't written, they're rewritten"
—R.C. Bannon

ONE OF the biggest mistakes that inexperienced songwriters make is to think their latest song is finished as soon as they've added the final chord or found a rhyme for the last line. The first draft could, of course, prove to be the one and the song may be ready for the demo studio. But in the majority of cases, 'finishing' a song is just the beginning.

It means it's time to start polishing the song to make it shine even brighter.

Professional songwriters recognize this. Experience has shown them that every new song they write will probably need several re-writes before they have the final version. They've learnt that creating a hit song usually requires 10% writing and 90% re-writing.

If you've already gone through the agony of having songs rejected by a publisher or a record company, ask yourself: Could I have made the songs better if I'd spent more time polishing them?

You should never allow yourself to be discouraged by the amount of re-writing and lyric editing that may be necessary. Look on it as simply part of the overall songwriting process.

Your aim should be to write great songs—not just settle for good ones.

Pro writers often produce a first draft of a new song, put it down for a few days, and then listen to it again. That's usually when they can tell if the song truly has potential. Listening to it from a fresh perspective enables them to spot the weaknesses and assess how the song can be improved.

"The A material definitely lies beneath the B material," the Goo Goo Dolls' Johnny Rzeznik once said. "You have to sift through it to get to the good stuff. You can't rush it. There is a time for your internal judge to come in and make the call, but you have to free yourself from that in the beginning stages of the creative process."

One of the purposes of this book is to give you a detailed checklist that you can measure your songs against, no matter how 'finished' you think they are. The aim is to help you improve each new song by making sure you haven't made any fundamental mistakes at each key stage in the development of the song.

# # # #

#85
NOT MAKING A 'MEMO' DEMO

YOU MAY have sung your latest song a hundred times in your writing room or while performing it live on stage. But it is often hard to spot any remaining flaws in the song's structure when you're busy concentrating on playing your instrument and trying to give a good vocal performance.

If the first time you get to listen back to a recording of your song is when you're already in a professional demo studio, you could end up wasting expensive studio time by having to make last-minute adjustments to the song.

The best way to judge whether a song is truly finished is to hear it back just like an ordinary listener. In other words, listen to it without singing or playing along. Just your ears and a lyric sheet.

To do this, you need to make a simple recording of your new song—in effect, a rough 'demo' of the demo recording that you intend to make.

"I recommend that writers record all the time," said The Kinks' Ray Davies. "When you're writing, you're doing this balancing act between the instinctive thing that leaps right out of you and the refinement of that moment. The first time you sing a line, you might use a weird phrasing, or put a line on the upbeat rather than on the downbeat. Shifts like that will change everything, and you have to document what you did … You can always play the tape and say, 'Oh, that's how I did it!'."

This 'memo' demo should be an essential part of the re-writing and editing process. It can be as basic as a simple guitar/vocal or piano/vocal captured on a hand-held digital recorder or a smartphone.

During the re-writing process, you should re-record and listen back to your rough recording every time you make more changes to the lyrics or melodic structure. You'll be amazed how it gives you a different perspective on how the song can be improved.

Once you're absolutely satisfied with the song and your final test recording, you'll then have something to play to the musicians and the vocalist (if you're not planning to sing it yourself), so that they can learn the song in advance … and save you time and money in the studio.

# # # #

#86
HEY BUDDY, CAN YOU SPARE SOME TIME?

UNLESS YOU'RE writing for your own band, or collaborating with other writers, songwriting can be a solitary endeavor. You're left alone in your writing room day after day, night after day, fighting the twin demons of indecision and procrastination.

As Steve Forbert once put it: "The most annoying thing about songwriting is that you just have to put in the solitude and the time it takes to get it done. It requires a lot of alone time."

That's why it can be very useful to have a songwriting buddy.

Your buddy could be a musician friend or a fellow songwriter you respect and trust—someone who will give you a chance to think out loud and be a sounding board for your new ideas. Ideally, your buddy should be someone who understands songwriting and whose encouragement, experience and insight will help you gain momentum and confidence in your own writing.

Writers are often not the best judges of their own material, regardless of their level of experience or success. They often get so close to a song that it is hard for them to tell if it is truly finished or still has some weaknesses.

At the crucial re-writing stage, your songwriting buddy can provide unbiased feedback before you start spending hard-earned cash on a demo, or putting in the hours in your home recording studio. He or she can give you valuable criticism or informed praise from an outside perspective, and point out what still isn't working in your song.

If you don't know any experienced songwriters, your buddy could always be a special person that you trust—such as your girlfriend, boyfriend, best friend, husband or wife. Someone you can take your stripped down 'memo' demo to—without feeling embarrassed or self-conscious—and ask for an honest opinion of the song.

# # # #

#87

BEYOND REASONABLE DOUBT

DON'T MAKE the mistake of shying away from the tough decisions that often have to be made at the re-writing stage—especially when strengthening a song means having to change or leave out some of the favorite lyrics, rhymes, melodic phrases, chords, or even complete verses that you started out with.

But you have to be ruthlessly honest with yourself. If you feel the song is the absolute best you can do beyond reasonable doubt (as they say in court), then go ahead and submit the song. But if you have the slightest doubt, you must be prepared to focus on identifying the song's weaknesses (and fix them) before spending time and money on making a demo.

If you aren't willing to re-visit or re-work your songs and do whatever is best for each of them, then the rejection slips may continue to pile up in your letter-box. A song that is 'close enough' for performing on stage won't be good enough for publishers, A&R managers and producers who have to operate in the tough commercial world of the music business.

Re-writing and editing can be hard work. You have to do it without losing the spontaneity and spark of inspiration that gave you the idea for the song in the first place. It may require finding a fresh way of saying what you want to say in your song, or correcting some of the common mistakes highlighted in this book. But it's essential step if you want songwriting success.

As mentioned previously in this book, an easy method of monitoring your progress during the re-writing stage is to make a simple guitar/vocal or piano/vocal recording on a hand-held recorder or a smartphone every time you make adjustments to the song. Hearing the song back like an ordinary listener will give you a different perspective on the changes you've made and may highlight any remaining flaws in the song.

'Polishing' a song is one of the most crucial steps in writing a hit, so it's better to take your time and keep re-writing and editing until you feel the magic happen … and the song finally falls into place beyond reasonable doubt.

# # # #

PART 5:

RECORDING YOUR DEMO

#88
NOT SEEING YOUR DEMO AS A SELLING TOOL

IF YOUR ambition is to earn money from songwriting, it's important to remember that a demo is more than just a permanent recording of your song for posterity. A demo is the advertisement for your song. It's your billboard.

Like any advertisement you see on TV or in a magazine, your demo has to be able to attract people's attention and stimulate their interest. Most importantly, IT HAS TO SELL.

Just like any other business, you have to invest in marketing and selling your wares. A demo is your most important sales and marketing tool—whether you're trying to get a record deal for your band or yourself as a singer-songwriter, or offering your song to a music publisher, or pitching your songs direct to producers.

So it is crucial to spend time getting it right.

Most publishers, A&R reps and producers are busy people who continually work under pressure. You may only be able to get them to listen to your demo once. That means it has to make an immediate impression and hit them right between the eyes (or, preferably, between their ears) first time around.

In the advertising world, they give each brand a 'USP' (a unique selling point) in order to differentiate it from rival brands. In effect, the message of every ad you see is: "Buy this product and you'll get this specific benefit" (the USP).

You have to make sure that your demo conveys your USP. It has to show publishers and record labels how they will benefit if they 'buy' into your songs and sign you up.

Whether you make a demo with your own home recording set-up or in a professional studio, the recording needs to measure up to the highest quality standards expected by music industry pros. But that doesn't mean it has to be an expensive, full-band studio production with all the frills.

If the demo is designed to sell the song itself, it doesn't require much production. It just needs to sound professional. All you need is a solid and tight rhythm track with a strong lead vocal that stays in tune. The vocal should be upfront in the mix so that listeners can hear the lyrics clearly. However, a good song should still stand out even if the demo only features one voice and a single piano or guitar.

An artist demo for a record label usually requires a little more production to showcase your sound and originality. It doesn't have to be as polished as a finished record, but it must demonstrate your performance intensity, emotion, depth of musical substance ... and your star potential.

If you're a singer-songwriter or in a band, video demos are now a relatively low-cost option for getting your material noticed.

Many publishers and A&R reps now regularly search YouTube for new writers and artists. Lana del Rey, for example, was discovered and signed by Interscope Records after John Ehmann, the company's senior director of A&R, spotted her video for 'Diet Mountain Dew' on YouTube.

But you have to apply the same quality criteria to a video demo as you do to an audio demo. Your footage won't impress an A&R exec if it looks amateurish and the sound quality is terrible. So don't just shoot it on a smartphone and upload it. Many recording studios now offer a video facility as well as audio recording. So use the best audio-visual technology you can afford to showcase your style and sound, and most importantly the song itself.

Remember, you're running your own small business, so you need to take a risk and invest in the stuff you're selling in order to make money from it. But, as mentioned earlier in this book, your product (your song) has to be right... and the quality of your audio or video demo has to make you look and sound like a pro.

# # # #

#89
SPENDING GOOD MONEY ON BAD SONGS

AS A publisher, I have often received song demos that were clearly expensive studio recordings featuring professional session musicians. The demos were often excellent productions that sounded like masters. In many cases, though, I still passed on them because the songs themselves just weren't good enough.

If you really believe in your talent and you're willing to spend a small fortune on your demos, that's fine. But you shouldn't even think of rushing into a studio until you've got the most important ingredient right—the song itself. It has to be as polished and shiny as you can make it, otherwise you could be wasting your money.

Publishers, A&R executives and producers would rather hear a potential hit song in its rawest voice/piano or voice/guitar form than waste their time listening to a demo of an average song hidden behind great engineering or great production.

So don't spend good money on demos of bad songs. You have to accept that not every song you write will be worthy of a demo.

And don't fool yourself into thinking that something magical will happen in the studio and your rusty piece of metal will suddenly be turned into gold. An average song will always be an average song, no matter how well studio musicians dress it up.

Ask friends or relatives, or a songwriting buddy, for their honest opinion of the song that you want to demo. Sing it for them accompanied by just a piano or a guitar.

If you can't make the song sound special in such a raw, stripped-down form, then it probably isn't worth spending your hard-earned cash on making a studio demo of it.

# # # #

#90
RELYING ON A DEMO TO FIX A SONG

UNLESS YOU have your own home recording set-up where you can afford to experiment with demos, don't make the mistake of taking a new song into a professional studio believing you can fix any structural weaknesses during the demo recording process.

When you've booked a studio for a certain number of hours—and the studio clock keeps on ticking—there's a huge amount of stress and pressure in the room. It's like taking a crucial test at school and you're working against the clock and starting to panic. Unless you're in a successful band with all the studio time in the world, it's not the ideal environment for trying to perfect a song.

So don't waste expensive studio time on trying to fix a problem that should really have been resolved at the re-writing and polishing stage.

When you have a brand new song and you're really excited about it, there is understandably a temptation to rush into the nearest studio and demo it right away—even if there are still one or two cracks in the song. Much better to be patient and spend a little more time getting the song right before you enter a studio.

Hit songwriter Max Martin, for example, sets a very high standard of quality-control for his songs which results in only one idea in 300 getting to the demo recording stage. "Sometimes you have to be a mass murderer and kill your darlings," he told *Time* magazine.

You can save yourself a lot of wasted time and money by making simple guitar/vocal or piano/vocal 'memo' demos on a hand-held recorder or a smartphone at the re-writing stage. Once you're satisfied with the song, you'll be able to play your final rough recording of it to the session musicians and demo vocalist (if you're not singing it yourself).

However, if you still have any doubts about the song before going into the studio, don't think giving it the full demo treatment will solve the problem. It probably won't.

Most songs will, of course, sound better with the help of a full studio production and professional musicians. But experienced publishers and A&R executives will look behind the production façade—and all the fancy guitar fills and background vocals—and spot any remaining flaws in the song itself.

# # # #

#91
NOT KNOWING WHAT YOU WANT BEFORE GOING INTO THE STUDIO

UNLESS YOU'RE highly adept at getting the best out of digital home recording software and equipment, you may have to book a session at a professional recording studio if you want a good-quality demo. And quality studio time doesn't come cheap.

One of the most expensive mistakes that many new songwriters make is to go into a demo studio without having a clear idea of what they want in terms of the arrangement, instrumentation, sound and feel.

If you aren't singing the song yourself, you could eat up valuable studio time trying to establish the best key for the singer, and then have to transpose all your chord charts and other musical parts into the singer's key.

If you haven't already written a catchy melodic phrase or riff for the intro section, more time could be wasted if you have to wait for the guitarist or keyboardist to adlib a suitable intro.

Similarly, if you haven't created all your secondary hooks in advance, you could lose more studio time if you have to rely on the musicians to come up instrumental, rhythmic or other sound hooks.

It is essential for time-consuming elements such as these to be carefully planned before you set foot inside the studio.

A recording studio can be a high-pressure environment, and writers who are just starting out often feel a little overwhelmed and intimidated. If you end up experimenting with ideas instead of recording tracks, the only person who will benefit is the studio owner because you'll have to pay for the extra studio time.

If there is a cap on the studio time available to you, you could end up rushing the recording because you're running out of time. This invariably results in a demo that you're not 100% happy with. And, for years to come, it will always bug you that the demo could have been so much better if only you had been better organized during the session.

# # # #

#92
FAILING TO MAKE AN IMPACT

SOME NEW writers make the mistake of submitting a demo even though they know the sound quality isn't great. They assume that publishers, A&R reps and producers will take the time to imagine what the song would sound like if it had been recorded in a studio or with better-quality home recording gear.

In reality, most music industry pros are just too busy to do that. While they aren't necessarily looking for the best studio quality in a demo, what they hear does subconsciously influence their attitude to a song.

When they press 'play' and hear a poorly recorded voice/piano or voice/guitar demo, they will instantly assume you're an amateur—and they will expect your songs to be amateurish too.

Some less generous music industry execs will immediately hit the 'stop' button because they don't want to waste their time on amateurs. Others (usually the decent folks who started out as aspiring songwriters just like you) may give your demo another 30-60 seconds to make an impression.

It is therefore vital to produce the best-sounding demo you can afford in order to make an impact on the listener within the first few bars—even if it means waiting a few more weeks until you've got enough cash to make a decent recording that will do your song justice.

Be aware, though, even expensive studio recordings don't always produce the demo quality that you want. This is usually because the session ends up being rushed.

That's why it's important to plan a demo carefully and well in advance. A few days before the session, give the musicians and singers a copy of your rough 'demo' demo, along with a chord chart and lyric sheet. This will give them time to learn the song before coming into the studio (and before the studio clock starts counting down the precious session time you've booked!).

If you can't afford a full studio demo with drums, bass and 'color' instruments like electric guitars and keyboards, a stripped-down voice/piano or voice/guitar demo can still help you sell your song—provided the sound quality is good (with no pops or hiss or dropouts).

Simply adding vocal harmonies and handclaps to a single-instrument demo will help to increase the impact on the listener. It will make the production sound 'bigger' without having to spend your hard-earned cash on other instruments and musicians!

# # # #

#93
YOUR DEMO IS OVER-PRODUCED

AT THE other end of the scale from a poorly recorded demo is the song demo that is over-produced.

With the spread of affordable digital recording software and equipment, many demos tend to be as good as masters these days. But don't make the mistake of recording a demo that is so busy and over-crowded that the most important ingredient—the song itself—gets lost in a forest of multi-layered instruments and vocals.

Sound quality and sounding professional are very important, of course. But sometimes less is better than more—otherwise there's a risk of your demo appearing sloppy because there's way too much going on.

You should avoid this trap if you're trying to land a record deal. At the demo stage, record labels aren't really interested in hearing amazing guitar solos, drum fills and production gimmicks. They're looking for self-contained artists who write great songs (and hit singles) and have a unique sound.

If the purpose of the demo is to pitch your song for someone else to record, a full production can sometimes hinder rather than help. It is often better to leave plenty of room for a producer or an artist to imagine how they would record the song if they like it. If the demo version is too complete, they may not be able to hear it done any other way. And if the way you've recorded it is not their style, they may simply reject the song.

A good-quality scaled-down demo can give you much greater flexibility, and may allow you to pitch the same song to artists in different genres. It will also make it easier for a music publisher to see the song's versatility.

That's why experienced writers often record both a full band demo and a scaled-down voice/guitar or voice/piano version—especially if the song is a ballad.

Country music legend Don Williams is just one artist who prefers to hear new songs performed by the writer with just a guitar or piano. "Demos can go one of two ways for you," he once said. "If it's a demo that helps, sometimes it'll help a lot. But by the same token, I think there are demos that close the door because it takes you in a direction that maybe you don't want to go in."

He added: "It'll color the attitude you might have about the song. Without the demo you might have viewed it another way."

# # # #

#94
VOCALS AND LYRICS AREN'T CLEAR

HOW OFTEN have you seen a product advertisement in a magazine that simply displays a picture and does not include any words that explain what the product is called, what it does, and what its unique selling point is?

In the case of a brand new product that nobody has ever heard of, such a vague ad would probably generate zero sales.

As mentioned previously in this book, a demo is an advertisement for a song that nobody has ever heard before. So the same sales and marketing criteria apply.

People need words to tell them the title and what the song is all about so that they can decide whether or not to buy it.

This means a demo has to sell your lyrics as well as the music—so the lead vocal has to be upfront in the mix to enable listeners to hear the words clearly.

Getting a hot mix is a critical part of producing a professional-sounding recording. But all you need on a good demo is a solid and tight rhythm track with a strong lead vocal that stays in tune. The music should never be allowed to drown out the singer.

Bear in mind that the people you submit your demo to are unlikely to hear the track for the first time on studio-quality speakers. Most of the publishers, A&R people and producers that I know usually listen to new demos in the car, on an MP3 player while commuting, on a laptop or mobile device, or on a small audio system in the office.

That's why it is always best to mix your demo down to small speakers.

And if someone is listening to the demo while travelling, they probably won't have a copy of the lyrics with them—so even more reason to make sure the vocal and the lyrics are crystal clear.

If they have to strain to hear the words, they may just hit the 'stop' button ... and move on to someone else's demo.

# # # #

#95
TO SING OR NOT TO SING

DON'T MAKE the mistake of singing the lead vocal on your demo if you're not really a singer. You have to be brutally honest with yourself and ask: Does my voice sound professional enough to help sell the song? Or am I better at writing tunes than singing in tune?

Obviously, if you're writing for your own band and you have a great lead singer—or if you're nurturing a talented new band or solo artist—then projecting the song through their vocals shouldn't be a problem.

However, if the purpose of your demo is to secure a publishing contract or to pitch a song to a producer, you shouldn't try to cut corners by singing on the demo yourself—especially if you know the vocals won't be as good as they need to be, or if your voice just won't be right for this recording.

If you really believe in the song, you may have to invest in hiring a professional session singer to highlight the song's true quality and hit potential. If you can't afford to do that, maybe you have a friend who can sing in tune and phrase and enunciate words well. Either way, it's essential to find the right singer for the song.

If you're making a stripped-down voice/piano or voice/guitar demo (as opposed to an informal rough demo), the quality of the vocal becomes even more important because it is completely exposed for all to hear. The voice carries the entire responsibility for creating a positive first impression when a publisher or A&R rep hears the song.

Even if it's a full studio demo, you can't try to hide a poor lead vocal in the mix. As mentioned in the previous section, the voice always has to be upfront to enable listeners to hear the words clearly and to help sell your lyrics as well as the music.

# # # #

#96
WRONG VOCAL STYLE ON THE DEMO

IF YOU'RE not a singer, and you need someone else to provide the lead vocals on your demo, make sure you choose a vocalist with a sound and style that is compatible with the song.

If you don't, there's a danger that any mismatch between the singer and the feel of the track could weaken the demo's ability to sell the song.

You first have to choose the music genre that best suits the song—e.g. pop, rock, dance or country—and decide if the song requires a male or a female singer. The next step is to find a vocalist who is comfortable with this type of music, has the right voice for it, and can capture the essence of the song.

You also have to make sure that your rough 'memo' demo gives the session singer a good idea of how you want the vocal to sound (no matter how good or bad your own voice may be!).

If the purpose of your demo is to pitch a song to an established artist, don't make it too hard for people to imagine the artist performing the song. Even if it is a potential hit and a perfect fit for the artist, don't expect a busy producer or A&R manager to take the time, for example, to translate the crooning style of the singer on your demo to the raunchy vocals of their R&B artist!

To make your song believable, the vocal style on the demo should be as close as possible to that of the artist you're targeting.

Any suggestion of incompatibility in the vocals could obscure the quality of the song itself—and may result in a rejection letter.

# # # #

#97
DON'T LET YOUR EGO GET IN THE WAY

IF YOUR demo is intended to sell the song itself—rather than provide a showcase for a band or you as a singer-songwriter— don't make the mistake of thinking that the quality of the musicianship doesn't really matter.

Poor musicianship on a demo is likely to make a good song sound inferior.

Don't expect to get away with saving money by playing on the demo yourself if you're fairly limited as a musician.

If your strength is writing songs rather than playing them, it may not be worth the savings if you skimp on quality musicians who could otherwise light up the song and enhance it with some brilliant playing.

As mentioned earlier in this book, while publishers, A&R reps and producers aren't necessarily looking for the best studio quality in a demo, what they hear does subconsciously influence their attitude to a song. So it's important to make sure your demo sounds professional—with a solid and tight rhythm track that keeps time, no slipped chords, and no bum notes in the guitar and piano fills!

And if the demo only features one voice and a single piano or guitar, it is doubly important that the playing is of the highest quality because every element of the recording will be exposed.

So be ruthlessly honest with yourself, and don't let your ego get in the way.

Do you really think you're competent enough to go into a high-pressure studio environment and play on the demo yourself? If not, it may be better to ask some experienced musician friends to do you a favor. Or, if you really believe in the song, consider hiring professional musicians if you can afford it.

Working with the right musicians is an essential ingredient if you want to end up with a good recording that will create a positive first impression for your song.

# # # #

#98
PUTTING AN INSTRUMENTAL BREAK IN YOUR DEMO

IF THE purpose of your demo is to get your song picked up by a music publisher, A&R manager or a record producer, all they want to hear is the quality of the song—so don't make the mistake of including a long instrumental section that doesn't add anything to the song itself.

It's okay to include a short instrumental hook or riff in the intro, or as a distinctive musical link between the end of the chorus and the start of the next verse. But a long, gratuitous guitar solo is not going to impress anyone and is unlikely to convince them to sign your song.

Obviously, if your aim is to secure a record deal for yourself or your band, an artist demo usually requires a little more instrumentation to showcase your sound, style and originality. But only include an instrumental break if you feel you need to demonstrate your musicianship or your potential as a live performer.

Keep it short though—ideally about four bars and no longer than eight. A two-minute solo or extended instrumental outro may simply test the listener's patience!

# # # #

#99
NOT TAILORING A PITCH DEMO

IF YOUR aim is to try to get a specific artist to record your song, you will have a better chance of success if your demo makes it easy for people to imagine the artist performing the song.

Not only does the song have to be tailored musically and lyrically to suit the artist that you're targeting, it's also important to personalize the arrangement on the demo so that it is as close as possible to the basic style of the artist.

That means taking time to analyze the artist's previous hits and, most importantly, his or her (or their) vocal range and favored keys. You should also study the arrangements of other songs recorded by the artist, and try to emulate that sound on your demo.

If the artist you're targeting is female, then the lead vocal on your demo should obviously be female.

If the artist is a dance-oriented pop star, the demo needs good beats ... and shouldn't sound country! And if you're pitching to a vocal group with several lead singers, take the sound of each singer into account.

Of course, tailoring a pitch demo doesn't mean making a full, multi-instrument studio recording that sounds as good as one of the artist's own tracks. You only need to produce it to the point where it will make a producer, A&R manager or a publisher sit up and take notice. It should help them to judge whether the song could work for the artist.

If they feel your song has strong potential, they may then take your demo to the next level and play it for the artist.

# # # #

PART 6:

OUTRO

#100
FORGETTING YOU'RE IN THE MUSIC BUSINESS

IF YOU want to earn your living as a writer, it's important to remember that songwriting is a business—not a hobby.

The experienced songwriters you'll be competing with are, in effect, running their own businesses ... and they've learnt the importance of being professional and reliable in everything they do.

That means you have to get your act together and be well-organized and self-disciplined too. Your 'customers' (publishers, A&R executives, producers, artists) need to know they can count on you.

If you promise to do something, do it.

The same criteria apply if you plan to sell your music direct to fans through your own website or via online music retailers such as iTunes, Amazon and CDBaby.

You need to establish a well-organized sales and marketing plan—and stick to it.

Make sure the way you interact with everyone is clear and professional—from face-to-face contact or telephone calls, to your letters, emails and text messages. And when communicating in writing, always double check your spelling, punctuation and grammar—otherwise you'll look like an amateur.

Stay organized by keeping all of your correspondence and important documents (such as contracts) in separate folders—ideally with a different color code for each folder category so you can find them easily. And make sure you keep your folders and demo masters in an efficient filing system.

Always be on time for meetings. If you're late without a very good reason, it suggests you don't care enough. Letting people down can harm your chances of getting a songwriting or recording deal, or placing your song with an important producer or artist. Arriving on time shows you are respectful, keen and reliable.

You're in the music business … so be business-like in all your dealings.

# # # #

#101
THE END OF THE BEGINNING

"This is not the end. It is not even the beginning of the end. But it is, perhaps, the end of the beginning"
—Winston Churchill

OKAY, SO you've finished a bunch of new songs. You've checked each one against all of the common songwriting mistakes highlighted in this book, and you've re-written and polished the songs so lovingly that they now sparkle like true gems. You've even recorded demos that you believe do the songs justice.

Some inexperienced writers make the mistake of thinking that, having got this far, they've done the hard part. In reality, though, now is when the real work begins.

As the great self-promoter Irving Berlin once said: "Talent is only the starting point…".

The next step in your development as a hit songwriter is what often separates talented writers from successful writers. What happens now can make the difference between recognition and success … or failure and anonymity.

There are two types of talented songwriters. Those who are so self-confident that they feel they deserve success and believe the music industry will eventually beat a path to their door. And those who are prepared to work hard and doggedly go out and market their songs to publishers, record labels, producers and artists.

Which category are you in?

In my experience, the only talented writers who have a real chance of achieving success are those who also possess a high level of determination, persistence, optimism and positive thinking (and a thick skin to cope with any rejection letters).

As Jimmy Webb once said: "You have to have persistence and tenacity to keep knocking on those doors. The people who are successful in songwriting always keep trying."

Diane Warren agrees: "You've got to believe if you're going to do this," she once said. "Believe in yourself, believe in your work."

Provided you think big, stay committed to your dream, and keep pushing hard enough, great songs will always find a home.

Some reports suggest that at least 100,000 new songs are released every week. With so much intense competition out there, you have to be able to stand out from the crowd.

That's why, at this stage, it's all about putting together a comprehensive marketing plan for your music—and sticking to it. There's no point in having an impressive collection of potential hit songs unless the right people get to hear the songs.

Good marketing is as important to you and your songs as it is to any brand in your local supermarket. It will get you noticed and encourage publishers and A&R reps to take you seriously.

As Kenny Gamble of the Gamble & Huff songwriting team once said about achieving success as a songwriter: "It's a very blessed thing when it happens."

Best wishes for great success with all your songwriting endeavors!

# # # #

CHECKLIST

—Do you have a positive attitude toward your songwriting and your songwriting ambitions?

—Do you believe in yourself, your talent, and your ability to succeed?

—Are you willing to work hard and be determined and persistent, whilst preparing yourself for any knocks and disappointments that may come your way?

—Have you written your 'Job Description'? Are you clear about what kind of writer you aspire to be?

—Have you considered whether you may need to work with a collaborator?

—Have you established a daily writing schedule and are you sticking to it?

—Have you chosen a special writing place where you can focus and be creative?

—Have you set yourself daily, weekly and monthly objectives and deadlines?

—Have you laid solid foundations for your creative process?

—Are you well-organized so that you won't let great ideas and good opportunities get away?

—Have you compared your writing style with the latest hit songs to make sure it sounds current?

—Are you doing more than simply imitating songs that are already out there?

—Are you confident that what you're offering is what music companies want?

—How does your song compare with the kind of records that are currently being played on radio?

—Are you confident that your song will have broad consumer appeal?

—Is your song a potential single? (remember, don't write 'album tracks'!)

—If your song is for an established artist, have you fully researched the artist's style and musical influences to make sure your song is appropriate?

—Are you confident that your song can pass the 12 tests that will decide its fate?

—Are you confident that you have achieved a good balance in the shape and form of your song?

—Have you analyzed the structure and key sections of today's biggest hits and compared them with your own song?

—Have you identified the key elements of current hits, learnt how they work, and applied this knowledge to your own song?

—Have you avoided forcing the development of your song so that it comes to life in its own time?

—Will other people be able to relate to your song? Or is it too personal or self-indulgent?

—Are you confident that you have avoided over-writing your song and making it too complicated? Can it be remembered easily?

—Does the length of your song fit with current trends?

—Are all your verses the same length every time?

—Are all your choruses the same length every time?

—Does your song get to the first chorus and the hook in less than 60 seconds?

—Does your verse build musically and lyrically as a 'stepping stone' to the chorus?

—Are you confident that your song is distinctive enough to stand out from the pack?

—Are you convinced that your song can build an emotional connection with the listener?

—Is the structure of your song familiar enough so that listeners will feel comfortable with it, without the song being too predictable?

—Have you given your song a killer high point and put it in the right place within the song?

—Have you made sure your song is clearly focused on making only one major point from one point of view?

—Are you confident that your song title is strong enough to attract people's interest and so help you sell the song?

—Have you positioned the title in the right place within the song?

—Are you confident that you have made the melody line easy for people to remember?

—Have you made sure your key musical phrases are repeated often enough to make the song sound instantly 'familiar' and memorable?

—Are the repeated sections exactly the same each time they appear?

—Are you sure the mood and emotion of the melody is compatible with the lyrics? Do your words and music belong together?

—Have you made sure the song's melody range is not too wide and is within most singers' vocal range?

—Have you built in rests and pauses so that the singer has space to breathe?

—Is there sufficient melodic contrast between your chorus and the verses to make the chorus really stand out?

—Have you built a 'Call To Action' into your chorus?

—Are you sure you've chosen the best chords and chord progressions so that the song has a sense of harmonic direction?

—Have you experimented with minor chords and other 'unexpected' chords that add extra color, texture and character to the song?

—Have you made sure the notes, chords, and chord progressions in this song are not exactly the same as in your other songs? (otherwise they may all start to sound the same).

—Does your song include a memorable melodic hook that will get inside the listener's head?

—Are you confident you have positioned your melodic hook in the best place within the song?

—Have you also included a lyrical hook that will stick in the listener's mind?

—Are you sure the rest of the song is up to the same high standard as the melodic and lyrical hook?

—Have you also created secondary hooks to make the song even more memorable?

—Are you confident that your intro section is strong enough to attract attention and draw people into the song?

—Have you made sure your intro is not too long, so that the first verse starts within 15-20 seconds?

—Have you included a bridge section as a temporary 'release' from the repetition of the verses and chorus?

—Are you confident that you have built your bridge in the right place?

—Have you included a pre-chorus to help build tension and propel listeners into the chorus?

—Do you feel you've done enough to make the chorus stand out from the verses?

—Were the words written as lyrics rather than poetry?

—Have you paid as much attention to the lyrics as the melody?

—Are you confident that your lyrics work well within the form and structure of the song?

—Do your lyrics in the verses mostly use descriptive words, while the chorus lyrics express emotions?

—Have you avoided an imbalance in your lyrics by making sure corresponding lyric lines in the verse are the same length in every verse?

—Have you avoided an imbalance by making sure corresponding lyric lines in the chorus are the same length in every repeated chorus?

—Have you avoided putting too many words in your lyrics so that the singer has space to grab a breath?

—Do your lyrics paint a picture rather than simply convey information?

—Have you made sure the first line of the song is truly inventive and memorable so that it will have an immediate impact on the listener?

—Do your lyrics in the verse move the story forward rather than simply restate what has already been said?

—Have you avoided the use of clichés in your lyrics?

—Are your lyrics conversational and easy for people to relate to?

—Have you maintained a consistent viewpoint throughout the song?

—Have you made sure your use of tense is consistent throughout the song?

—Are your rhymes inventive and not too predictable?

—Have you varied your rhyming pattern in the verse, chorus and bridge, so that each section is different and has its own personality?

—Have you made sure the lyrics are easy to sing, and don't contain too many tongue-twisters?

—Have you gone through a comprehensive re-writing process to make sure the song is as strong as possible?

—Did you use the 'memo demo' technique of recording a rough review demo at each stage of the re-writing process?

—Are you confident that the song is the best you can do beyond reasonable doubt?

—Are you confident that the song is strong enough for you to spend time and money on it at the demo stage?

—Are you sure you have the final version of the song so you won't have to spend time making further changes at the demo stage?

—Have you made sure you know exactly what you want in terms of feel and sound before starting work on the demo?

—Have you been ruthlessly honest with yourself about whether your singing and playing are good enough for the demo?

—Have you made sure the song hasn't got lost in the production on the demo?

—Are the vocals and the lyrics clear on the demo?

—Are you sure you have the right vocal style on the demo?

—If you have included an instrumental break in the demo, are you sure it really adds something and needs to be there?

—If you have written the song for another artist, have you tailored the demo to suit the artist's style?

—Are you confident that you have made the song demo as impactful as possible so that you can use it as an impressive 'advertisement' and selling tool for your song?

—Have you put together a comprehensive marketing plan for your song?

# # # #

IF YOU'VE ticked most of the boxes above, then it looks like you're ready to roll.

Best wishes for great success with your songs.

And keep in mind these words from the late great US singer-songwriter Dan Fogelberg:

"You're successful if you can get one person to pick your song up and put it on the turntable and go, 'Wow, thanks for writing that!'."

# # # #

28084184R00099

Printed in Great Britain
by Amazon